chasing youth culture and getting it **right**

chasing youth culture and getting it right

how your **business** can **profit** by tapping into today's **most powerful** **trendsetters and** **tastemakers**

tina wells

WILEY

John Wiley & Sons, Inc.

Published by John Wiley & Sons, Inc., Hoboken, New Jersey.

Published simultaneously in Canada.

For general information on our other products and services or for technical support, please contact our Customer Care Department within the United States at (800) 762-2974, outside the United States at (317) 572-3993 or fax (317) 572-4002.

Wiley also publishes its books in a variety of electronic formats. Some content that appears in print may not be available in electronic books. For more information about Wiley products, visit our web site at www.wiley.com.

Library of Congress Cataloging-in-Publication Data:

Wells, Tina, 1980-

Chasing youth culture and getting it right : how your business can profit by tapping into today's most powerful trendsetters and tastemakers / Tina Wells.

p. cm.

ISBN 978-1-118-00405-0 (cloth)
ISBN 978-1-118-06155-8 (ebk)
ISBN 978-1-118-06156-5 (ebk)
ISBN 978-1-118-06166-4 (ebk)

1. Young consumers—United States—Attitudes. 2. Generation Y—United States—Attitudes. 3. Marketing. I. Title.
HF5415.332.Y66W45 2011
658.8'342—dc22

2010050403

Printed in the United States of America

10 9 8 7 6 5 4 3 2 1

Contents

Preface

I started my career almost 15 years ago, at the age of 16. I will admit it was a total and complete accident. At the time, I was working as a writer for a newspaper for girls out of New York City, *The New Girl Times*. The publisher of the paper, Miriam Hipsh, really gave me—and other young writers—an amazing opportunity. I really understood the power of my voice. What started out as a gig writing product reviews turned into a company I founded called The Buzz. The Buzz transformed into Buzzteen.com, which eventually became Buzz Marketing Group.

I've spent my entire career focusing on this concept of chasing youth culture and getting it right. From a very young age, I've had the privilege of working with brands like Verizon Wireless, Candie's, Maidenform, American Eagle Outfitters, PBS, and a host of others. I've been able to learn from the things they did right and also major blunders they've made in their efforts to satisfy the Millennial consumer.

We live in a world that is completely obsessed with staying young and understanding young people. This book isn't just for the marketers who are trying so hard to capture the youth dollar, it's for the Millennials' teachers, parents, the media—anyone who wants to understand how to talk to and understand today's young people.

I hope that, through this book, I will be able to finally put an end to a few Millennial myths (e.g., that they're apathetic, that they don't care about anything) and also enlighten you on how they behave and how they want to be communicated with (tribes are important, and you have to speak their language).

In this book you'll learn about mind-set marketing, and how you have to market to Millennials based on their tribal needs. Millennials want you to talk to them in a distinct way, and understanding what their needs are will make this communication that much easier. I'll also discuss the importance of technology and how it's changing the way Millennials think and feel about the future. It greatly impacts the way marketers communicate with them. Finally, I'll introduce the concept of *global mobiles*—my new name for Millennials. The world has truly become their oyster, and there are no technological limits when it comes to consuming the goods they really want.

I hope that you enjoy this book, and I hope that it serves as a guide to you on your journey to better understand Millennials. This book is full of advice that I give my clients every day. I believe that marketers truly want to understand Millennials—actually, we all do—and this book is my attempt to start what I hope is a very engaging and ongoing conversation. Let the conversation begin.

Acknowledgments

Writing this book has been a dream of mine for quite some time. Putting together a book like this—full of independent research—requires much more time and effort than I could have put forth on my own. For all of their help and guidance, I am eternally grateful to my team: Becky Cabaza, Sam Wilson, Adrianne Washington, and Marcus Wells.

My editor at John Wiley & Sons, Inc., Dan Ambrosio, through his insight and perception, made this book better than I had ever hoped it could be. Working with him inspired me every day.

I also have to thank my brilliant and long-suffering agent Kate Lee. She worked tirelessly and diligently to find me the right partner for this book. At one point, it truly became a labor of love. For that, I will be eternally grateful.

I am truly blessed to have fantastic clients. Every day, they inspire me with their thought-provoking ideas and innovations. I have been a part of their creative process for most of the past 15 years, and without those insights, this book would not have been possible.

Starting a company at 16 is not an easy feat, and I owe many thanks to a host of people for numerous kindnesses, whether it was an encouraging word, an idea, or an opportunity: Kathy Todaro-Hawn, Najma Nasir, Keith McCoy, Scott Cianci, Carol Elwell, Marianna Clark, Dr. Anita Jose, Dr. Kathy Lanegran, Dr. Courtney Carter, Dean Olivia White, Dr. Ronald J. Volpe, Professor Lawrence Gelburd, Frank Slattery, Andre Des Rochers, John Cunningham III, Dennis Wint, Mollie Slattery, Ross Martin, Dave Knox, Maria Dolgetta, Tonya Millard Stevenson, Rachel Williams and Ed Willis. You have all contributed so much to my professional and personal life, and for that I'm very grateful.

Above all, I'm grateful to the most loving and supportive family anyone could have. Your love and perseverance throughout my entire life—not only my career—has meant the most to me. No child could ever ask for more loving parents, no more loyal, loving, supportive siblings. Mom, Dad, Adrianne, Erica, Marcus, Lisa, and William, I love you so much, and this book is possible because of all of you.

To my niece Phoebe, I can't wait until you're old enough to read this book and give me feedback. And I certainly hope that my trend predictions are true. If so, you have an awesome life ahead of you.

To my amazing group of friends, thank you for keeping me sane throughout this process. You are all so supportive—and so talented in your own right. You inspire me every day, and I thank you for having me in your life. Kimberly, Tia, Stephanie, Michelle, Nurys, Jackie, Suny, Johnica, Sibyl, Abdallah, Melissa H., Melissa R., Tina P., David, and Diane, thank you all for being such great friends.

Finally, this book is for my buzzSpotters. I am indebted to all of you—more than 9,000 worldwide—who entrust me with your thoughts and opinions. It's because of that trust that I've been able to communicate on your behalf for all of these years. You amaze me. I am so inspired by who you are and who you want to become. I will always make it my cause in life to advocate for you. Thank you.

Part One

Introducing Generation 2.0

1

Meet the Kids

Say Hello to the Newest Wave of Millennials

Jamie's iPod alarm wakes her up with Miley Cyrus's "Can't Be Tamed." She throws back the sheets on her brand-new Target bed-in-a-bag, powers on her Sony Vaio laptop, and lets her friends (and the rest of the world) know that she's awake by updating her Facebook and Twitter profiles. After checking her Facebook newsfeed to see what her friends are up to, she grabs a pair of Olsenboye jeans, pairs them with a Material Girl top, and finishes off the look with classic Converse high-tops. She grabs her iPhone and sends a text message to her best friend to make sure their carpool to school is on time. She's already moving fast, and the day has just begun.

Meet Jamie—an everyday tween who represents the Millennial generation.

Pop Quiz

True or False: The majority of teens shop online.

BUZZFLASH: THAT'S A LOTTA KIDS

The U.S. Census Bureau estimates that within five years there will be more than 76 million American children under age 18. In 2015, the largest group of children will be between the ages of 5 and 13 (an estimated 39 million kids). There will be 17 million teenagers between the ages of 14 and 17, and 22 million kids under the age of 5. More than 20 percent of the total will be of Hispanic origin.

The term *Millennial* has become common parlance nowadays. It is usually used to describe a generation of young people who have changed the ways we think, work, and communicate. Although they're still in their formative years, members of this cohort have already made an impact on the entire planet through their innovative uses of technology, chaotic yet controlled attention spans, and constant craving for instant action and information. Although older generations may occasionally complain about these new ways of life, we all know that we indeed live in a new world and, like it or not, we will follow the Millennials' lead.

Who, exactly, are these Millennials? Basically, this group consists of anyone aged 8 to 26, born during the years 1984 to 2002. Breaking them down another level, Millennials are tweens, teens, and young adults. Chapter 2 describes ways to categorize young people based on their mind-set and preferences rather than age, but let's start with the numbers.

Tweens are Millennials between the ages of 8 and 12 (sometimes as old as 14) and, as far as marketers are concerned, are the most important age group in this generation for one significant reason: They spend their parents' money. They also have some cash of their own to spend. According to C&R Research, the average weekly allowance is $9. The bulk of their personal money comes from gifts from parents and grandparents. Of course, there are plenty of other reasons to focus heavily on tweens. They are the first age group of humans to grow up completely engulfed in a world connected by the Internet. They are learning in entirely new ways, and they will mature with a constantly evolving educational system. They'll be the first to use more electronic tools (computers, e-learning software, and touch-screen test taking) in the classroom than traditional ones like pencil and paper. All of these new tools allow tweens to learn faster than any generation before them, and therefore to find their identity and formulate their opinions at a much younger age than society is used to.

Tweens are essentially the "golden egg" for marketers, as capturing market share in this demographic can result in substantial payoffs. Consider the rise and continued popularity of a company like Disney. This entertainment corporation—at one time focused almost entirely on cartoons, films, and in-person entertainment like theme parks—has extended its brand in a variety of ways to remain in the forefront of the tween market. For example, the launch of the Miley Cyrus properties, starting with the Hannah Montana television series and extending Cyrus's musical products, exhibited Disney's role as a major player in the music business. Disney's record label, Hollywood Records, has experienced tremendous success and increased revenues while the rest of the major record labels are heading toward an inevitable demise.

Tween boys are a bit tougher for marketers to figure out. They're still a bit finicky with their decisions and not as quick to choose their tastes and preferences with the same amount of conviction as their female counterparts. This leads brands to launch campaigns that consist of more trial-and-error marketing. Even sports, once a sure bet to attract tween boys, has been fragmented due to the rise in popularity of several new sports—including those once considered "alternative," like skateboarding and snowboarding—and the revitalization of old classics like martial arts. Basketball, baseball, football, and soccer are no longer the only popular choices.

Ten years ago, the tween market didn't even exist. We would have called them "children" or "kids." But this emerging group, in between childhood and the teenage years, is where the money and hot products are. Tweens are the first group to live entirely wired lives. Later in this book, we're going to discuss the effects of a totally wired life and examine the expectations of this tween consumer. For now, it's important to understand that marketing to tweens is a slippery slope: Tweens don't want to be treated like children, but they still come attached with a purse-string-holding adult. So, how can marketers please both tweens and their parents? They should take a page out of the marketing book of tween retailer extraordinaire, Justice.

Justice opened its doors in 2004. Some of you may remember its predecessor, Limited Too, launched in 1987 by Limited Brands. The store offers the most cutting-edge tween clothing that is also Mom and Dad approved. But the real secret to the retailer's success is its monthly *catazine*, a catalog/magazine, in which girls can preview items that will be arriving in stores, read special content, and participate in contests and promotions. Each month, Justice ships more than 11 million catazines, whose readership among tween girls is greater than that of *Girl's Life, Seventeen,* and *Teen Vogue* combined. Justice has figured out the way to speak to tweens. More important, it has translated into sales. Even in a tough economy, parents are still spending money on their tweens. If you're looking for an entry point into the youth market, the tween consumer may just be the right target for you.

I believe that for a brand to be successful in the tween market, it must meet three essential needs of the tween consumer: aspiration, security, and acceptance. Justice offers all of these things. Tween girls want to be teen girls. That will never change. They want to dress like their favorite Disney and Nickelodeon stars. Justice offers skinny jeans, UGG-style boots, and graphic tees. The stores even offer cosmetics and spa products! It's the very definition of tween aspiration.

It's also important for tweens to shop in a comfortable environment. Justice stores offer tweens that security. They know that there will be no embarrassing moments, shopping among their teen counterparts. More important, there are no tween boys. It's important to understand that even though tweens aspire to be older, psychologically, they are more like children than they are teenagers. They still need and want their mom to play a major role not only in their buying decisions, but also in their lives. In a recent Buzz Marketing Group survey, Mom ranked number one as a confidant over teachers and friends.

Tweens also need to feel accepted. If a tween girl is going to try out a "punk" look, it's more likely that her group of friends (or her tribe) will also be trying out this look. Tween girls are figuring out who they are and what they want to be. They're still not sure of themselves. They are experiencing new things every day and have not yet totally defined who they are. Tweens will not try a brand that has not yet been vetted for the cool factor. Even a Queen Bee tween is most likely sporting well-known brands. It's just not a risk they're willing to take.

While tween girls identify themselves based on their retail choices, tween boys are not shoppers. Where will you find a tween boy? The obvious answer is playing with his video games. They may have abandoned the Legos they played with as boys for Lego Star Wars, the action video game that, according to *Wired* magazine, has sold more than 6.7 million copies. We know that boys like the action and escapism offered in video games, but what else do they like?

Books. That's right, tween boys are big readers. And no series is more popular with tween boys than Jeff Kinney's *Diary of a Wimpy Kid*. This series offers every element I mentioned earlier as being important to tweens: aspiration, security, acceptance. In some ways, they can relate to the main character in the series, Greg Heffley. Even though he may be a little nerdy, he's aspirational. He's a nerd who wins. There is security in the reading experience. It's something that tween boys own. It can also be as private or as public as they like. And *Diary of a Wimpy Kid* is cool with other tween boys and girls, having sold millions of copies.

Here's one final caveat: Tweens are not brand-loyal. That's right, of all of these subsets, tweens are the most elusive. One example of their lack of loyalty is the transition of all of the Limited Too stores to Justice. Same products, different name, same tween customer. Tweens weren't at all loyal to the Limited Too brand. It may have been a different brand name, but it offered the same aspiration, security, and acceptance.

Even so, tween retail is exploding right now. Teen retailer Aéropostale launched its tween brand, P.S., in 2009. In 2010, it has opened more than 40 stores, with plans to open five more before the end of 2010. American Eagle Outfitters also launched its 77kids brand online in 2008. In 2010, it opened a handful of stores. These new stores join longtime tween retailers Abercrombie & Fitch, which has more than 200 Abercrombie stores, and Gap, which operates more than 200 GapKids locations. In 2011, they currently have 35 P. S. by Aéropostale stores. As of 2011, there are nine 77kids stores, according to ae.com.

Teens are Millennials between the ages of 13 and 19 (born between 1991 and 1997); this age group receives the majority of the Millennial generation's spotlight. America has been fascinated by teen culture for the past few decades. Movies like *Back to the Future* and *The Breakfast Club*, now considered classics, provided a few early glimpses into teen culture. They highlighted, in humorous and entertaining ways, the quick changes that occur in the lives of this puberty-stricken age group stuck between childhood and adulthood.

The fascination with teens really started to explode in the late 1990s with musical groups like the Backstreet Boys, NSYNC, and female

Forever Popular Forever 21

Forever 21 was founded in Los Angeles 1984 by a South Korean couple, Dong-Won Chang and Jin Sook, under the name Fashion 21. By 1989, the couple had changed the name to Forever 21 and was operating 11 stores. The eleventh store was also the company's first mall-based store. In 1995, they opened a store in Miami, which was the first location outside of California. By 1997, they were operating more than 40 stores. Today, more than 450 stores operate under the Forever 21 umbrella, and 2008 revenues were reportedly $1.7 billion.

What's the secret to the chain's success? Despite competitors like Charlotte Russe, H&M, and Wet Seal, Forever 21 seems to be the most popular with teens, and now tweens, since unveiling a new tween-targeted collection. For starters, it's not affordable luxury. No, that was the cloud on which H&M floated into the American psyche. Forever 21 is all about fast fashion. For example, you admire a friend's dress, she tells you it's from Forever 21, you go the following week, and it's nowhere to be found. That is the key to Forever 21's success. Forever 21 is appointment shopping. You must get it before it's gone. There is nothing Millennials love more than an experience that feels exclusive and limited. Throw in value, and you are on the fast track to superbrand status. Target has learned a thing or two from Forever 21, with its exclusive and affordable collections.

Emerging brands should think about what they can learn from Forever 21's quick thinking on fast fashion.

pop icons Britney Spears and Christina Aguilera. These entertainers showed us that the teen dream was alive and kicking, as the whole globe watched them grow up. (In fact, almost all of these performers were brought up in the Disney "farm system" while participating in the Mickey Mouse Club.) Marketers also took notice as these groups created an explosion of merchandising opportunities that pushed teens into the driver's seat to guide cultural tastes from music toward fashion.

At the turn of the century (and millennium), teen culture was in full swing with the launch of teen titles like *Teen People, Elle Girl,* and *Teen Vogue.* The popularity of these magazines proved that teens had a strong voice and commanded the attention of peers, parents, and marketers alike. The entertainment industry has become flooded with teen movies, teen television shows, teen actors, and televised contests searching for the next big teen talent.

While it seems that America's fascination with teens will continue, it is important to remember that this group of Millennials—more than tweens and young adults—still struggle to find their identity and commit to lifestyle choices. They're more likely to timidly feel their way through their adolescent years before really capturing their individualism as they approach the brink of young adulthood.

Capturing the heart of a teen consumer is no easy task. They have completely different motivations than their tween and young adult counterparts. I believe that there are three things that matter to the teen consumer: inspiration, disruption, and value. Teens need to feel inspired by the brands in which they invest their time and money, which companies like Pepsi have shown they understand. Pepsi's latest cause-marketing masterpiece, "Pepsi Refresh Project," has created a viral marketing juggernaut. Consumers are asked to participate in a voting process by selecting their favorite nonprofit cause for microgrants. They are also able to submit their own funding ideas in several key areas, including arts and culture, health, food and shelter, and the planet. Almost 2 million people "Like" this on Facebook. But inspiration via cause-marketing strategies is not the only thing that's important to teens. Retailers like American Eagle Outfitters offer visual inspiration to teens, and brands like Apple—with cutting edge technology and upbeat advertisements—are incredibly rousing as well.

While the notion of disruption may seem a bit counterintuitive, it's necessary in order for teens to embrace a new brand. We often hear about the power of disruptive technology, and one example I love to use relates to digital downloading. When music companies decided to phase out singles, teens and young adults began sharing files illegally online—a practice that was eventually replaced by legal services such as iTunes and Amazon.com. No longer was it necessary to purchase a 14-track CD for the sole purpose of owning a single favorite song; consumers simply didn't have to pay for music they did not want. However, record labels were not prepared to deal with this, and they still have not recovered. Their initial strategy was to sue consumers, the majority of whom were minors, instead of focusing on solving their main problem by creating and distributing music consumers wanted.

This is a case where I believe disruption can also go a step further. Simply put, *disruption* literally means "an interruption or interference." It is about innovation and understanding where your brand fits into a consumer's mind-set. Teens literally need to be *interrupted* to pay attention to your brand.

Let's think for a moment about a teenager's typical day. Teenagers normally rise around 6 AM, or hit the snooze button, thereby throwing off the rest of their prep time for the day. They'll eat something for breakfast on the run (how nutritious that something is isn't clear), dress, and either drive to school or catch the bus. They'll spend eight hours interacting with friends (and hopefully learning something). Then they're off to sports, after-school activities, a part-time job, or some combination of these. They're finally back at home in the evening doing homework, chatting with friends online, and (maybe) watching some TV.

There's a lot going on throughout that day, and at some point, teenagers make a decision to either interact with your brand or not. Are they eating *your* breakfast cereal? Dressing in *your* clothes? Talking on *your* cell phone? Driving *your* car to school, or walking there in *your* brand of shoes? They're doing these things with *someone's* products, and how they decide what to use is a result of a series of choices—both their own and those of others. It could be Mom who ultimately plunks down the cash for the purchase, a friend who shares the "latest thing," or a team member who advises them on the apparel that will best improve their game. Whatever your brand can do to be disruptive—to make just enough noise to become relevant—is extremely important to this group of consumers.

Finally, you have to offer value. Business students, on writing their very first business plan, are told that they must offer a "value proposition." This is a simple statement that normally starts with something like, "We promise to . . ." and ends with something like ". . . give you the shiniest hair possible [the most stylish pair of shoes, the best fashion content]." But there is one ending that trumps all others: ". . . at a reasonable price." When it comes to teens, price matters—more than you think. It did even before the recession hit. You can only imagine how they feel about it now, in this postrecession era. Teens have tons of expenses: lower-priced commitments, like prom, clothes, and electronic devices, and the bigger-ticket items as well, with college and a car purchase looming. The list goes on and on. Value, indeed, is of the most importance these days. A recent TD Ameritrade survey found that 36 percent of teens would delay college because of the price.

Young adults are Millennials between the ages of 20 and 26 (born between 1984 and 1990), and they are the first group of Millennials to cross over from childhood to adulthood during the Internet age. The timing of their maturity makes this group somewhat oxymoronic; while they're very valuable, they're also potentially destructive in many marketers' eyes. On one hand, today's young adults have tremendous capacity to change the way we think and learn. They grew up with one foot (or one toe, depending on how you look at it) in the old school, but with their eyes on new ways of doing things. This grants them the knowledge to communicate with older generations, who need help getting up to speed in a faster world and marketplace, while also using these very skills to outperform older generations who grew up in a much different, and much slower, learning environment. Many young adults are using this to their advantage; for example, Facebook founder and billionaire at 26 Mark Zuckerberg was recently the youngest person named to the *Forbes* list of richest people in America.

I just pointed out how disruptive innovation affects tweens, but a great example of the impact of young adults on modern commerce is evident in the music industry as well. Once-popular music file sharing program Napster, developed in 1998 by 18-year-old Shawn Fanning, hit its peak around 2000. The program allowed young adults to crack the record labels' codes, making music accessible on a widespread—and *free*—platform. As many people know, the labels fought back hard—and not very diplomatically. What resulted was a decade of dramatic and tragic decline of the organized music industry, all because the traditional powerhouses weren't willing to listen to the Millennial generation. Like Zuckerberg, Fanning was "just another kid in a Boston dorm room" who changed the face of global culture forever.

As far as marketers are concerned, young adults have moved past the point where they can rely on their parents for extra cash. Because they have the least amount of disposable income compared to other Millennials, they're the most difficult for marketers to reach. Like their younger teen and tween counterparts, young adults are learning to adapt more quickly to globalization than older generations. Zuckerberg and Fanning have showed us that this group can make a global impact—and be extremely well compensated for it— without following a traditional career-building path. This means that they are more business-savvy, often making them more money conscious and very aware of the current economic climate.

In addition to entering the workforce and having a better understanding of the value of a dollar, young adults have fine-tuned their tastes and developed more precise spending habits. They may have to pinch pennies at times, but they know what they want. Most of them stick to the tribal characteristics they've developed in their teenage years, and they're saving what they can for their first big luxury purchase. Some of them, however, may decide to invest by starting a new business or developing a hobby into something that they can monetize and use to put some extra money in their pockets.

What do they expect from marketers and from the brands they love? I believe that the three most important things to young adults are reflection, commitment, and self-fulfillment. By this stage in their lives, Millennials are looking for brands not to define them, but to *reflect* who they are. The college years have helped them identify their tribe—whether a wired techie or hipster preppy—and discover what they like.

The good news is that young adults provide a great target for emerging brands. If these consumers already identify with hipster culture, it's clear that they will at least consider purchasing products or services from a new brand in this category. An interesting example of this is the web site Karmaloop.com, an online retailer that specializes in urban fashion. Founded in 2000 by Greg Selkoe, this once-small online retailer now has over 3.5 million visitors per month and more than 30,000 brand evangelists. In 2005, a bricks-and-mortar store opened up on famous Newbury Street in Selkoe's hometown of Boston. Karmaloop.com carries more than 150 different brands—some well known, like Puma, and others lesser known, such as Hellz Bells. But fashion isn't all that this company is about. In 2008, Karmaloop.com registered thousands of young people to vote. It's clear that Karmaloop is a reflection of its customers, just as much as it's an inspirational place for them to shop.

It's not enough these days for young adults to see themselves in the brands that they love. They also feel a commitment *from* those brands. Converse is an example of this. For over 100 years, Converse's commitment to its consumers has not changed. The company, which predated Nike, Puma, and Reebok, has always been cutting-edge. It's one of very few products that can instantly increase a purchaser's "cool factor." That commitment to style and substance has not been lost on its young adult fans. Converse is also one of only a handful of brands that has not decreased its "hip factor" by partnering with Target. In fact, this has only increased its ubiquity.

In order for young adults to commit to a brand, the brand must first firmly establish its identity and not waver—no matter what the current pop culture says you have to do or be. A brand like Converse, which has survived over 100 years and consistently attracted the same core consumer, has clearly developed and stuck to a compelling identity.

Since these older Millennials have grown up in a world full of causes to support, they expect their brands to take part in some form of cause marketing. But it's not just about the cause for these consumers; they themselves need to experience a sense of fulfillment from interacting with the brand. Doing so might be as simple as buying a book via Amazon 1-Click or reading an article on www.nytimes.com. Self-fulfillment is the most important element of any brand experience for young adults. Projects like FEED Africa, which not only provides a chic handbag but also a year's worth of meals to a child in Africa, satisfy a need to be both fashionable and philanthropic.

This trend even extends to politics. President Barack Obama attributes a lot of his success to young adult voters who desperately wanted change. This group saw in President Obama what they see in themselves: hope, opportunity, intelligence, commitment. It is incredibly important for Millennials to be able to believe in something greater than themselves. They unite around causes, ideas, concepts—anything that represents the bigger picture. President Obama ran his campaign so much like marketers run brands that he was actually awarded 2008 Marketer of the Year by *Advertising Age* magazine.

In an October 2010 Buzz Marketing Group Political Pulse survey, in which more than 1,000 young adults participated, a whopping 92 percent of those surveyed said they would be voting in the midterm elections. What's interesting is that only 29 percent of respondents are actually happy with the job the president is doing. Young adults aren't rallying around the president; rather, they're rallying around a cause that is important to them—having their voice heard.

Economic Awareness

Now that we know *what* Millennials want from their brands, the bigger question is, given this economy, what can they *afford*? Historically, Millennials don't bring to mind a generation of people who need to save money. Yet these days, it's all about saving, and their priorities have definitely changed.

Our recent survey found that clothing was the number one casualty, followed by dining out, shoes, electronics, and movies, in that order. All of these correlate to companies that have suffered during this recession, with the exception of movies. In a recession, people need escapism. Whether it's TV, films, or happenings in pop culture, Millennials, and all of us, need an outlet for anger and frustration.

Almost everyone is worried about money. Those who don't have much are in a constant struggle to keep up. Those who do have some savings are holding on to what they have, waiting for more prosperous times. Millennials are no different. In the spring of 2010, we performed a recession-focused survey that revealed information on teen spending habits, changes in leisure-time activities, and the Millennial generation's hopes and worries for the future.

Tweens are the only group within the Millennials who, because they still completely rely on their parents for spending money, are experiencing little direct change in their spending habits, as exhibited in the following survey response: "My grandmom still gives me money all the time!" However, many of their parents are not earning as much as they used to and are more reluctant to dip into savings, so tweens feel a secondary impact.

While tweens have a lot of influence, there is still a major shift occurring with these consumers. According to Research and Markets, tweens spend $43 billion annually, which translates to about $2,047 per tween. This group's influence is everywhere, from automobile purchases to grocery store purchases. According to a recent Experian Research National Kid Study, kids have more influence over the brand of toothpaste used by their family (92 percent) than the toys they play with (82 percent). Additionally, 78 percent of tweens go grocery shopping with their parents, with girls (82 percent) outnumbering boys (68 percent).

Tweens still wield some power and influence in their households, but I believe that in this postrecession era, parents are taking back the power of the purse. This is more practical than psychological. There is simply less money to go around, and for the most part, moms have to allocate all of the household dollars.

Parents still feel the need to provide for their tweens in the same way that they may have provided for older teen and young adult siblings, so they're feeling the effects of the recession a bit less than their sibling counterparts, but their mom's influence is there.

Although tweens have yet to reach the age where they must adapt their behavior to the economy, 85 percent of the teen and young adult respondents to our survey say that their spending habits have changed because of the recession.

Teens are still bridging the gap between relying on their parents and finding jobs of their own (at least part-time jobs), and they're aware of the impact on both their parents and the job market. They exhibited a keen awareness regarding the shortage of cash these days, as shown in these responses: "When my mom is making less, then I get less," and "Getting a job is not as easy as it used to be." We can still expect teens to spend money, but this already-fickle demographic will become more and more choosey. This, of course, means marketers will have to work harder to sincerely engage with teens as they start to choose their preferences (likely to match the tribe that they're joining).

Our survey indicates that malls are getting quieter, because buying clothes is the number one casualty of the recession as it pertains to Millennial shopping habits. Malls are teen hangouts, so this doesn't mean that teens aren't shopping at all, but it adds pressure on marketers used to a youthful shoppers with a "this *and* that" mentality, evident during better times, who have switched to a "this *or* that" mind-set during the current economic malaise.

What's more, teens are turning to mall alternatives such as clothing swaps, eBay, and discount stores like Plato's Closet. Accessibility is so important to teens. It doesn't matter *how* they acquire a coveted item; it just matters that they get it, and in a timely fashion. This is why retailers like H&M and brands like Coca-Cola consistently rank high on brand index surveys. Teens—or the Microwave Generation, as I like to call them—need instant access.

In the survey, some teens even provided responses that business leaders and politicians of the past decade could have considered, such as, "Steady income is never a guaranteed thing, and . . . I should always plan ahead and save for a financial crisis." This leads teens to "think before [they] spend" and to move away from frivolous extra purchases (little things by the checkout, for instance) that have helped marketers retain market share.

Young adults, most of whom have outgrown the age of financial dependence, have learned the value of the dollar, unlike many previous generations. A lot of them are working and going to school at the same time, and many of them have significant student loan debt. The ones who spent their teens spending loosely have really pulled back the reins and learned to cope without the extras. Here's one response that shows a drastic shift from the past few decades of decadence and luxury: ". . . I can live without whatever it is I think I need, especially media. I can always borrow things from other people or find alternative ways of getting things, like from the library." In short, young adults have "learned to be more frugal" and now "look for quality and durability in the products [they] buy as opposed to trendiness or fancy packaging."

Not surprisingly, the Millennials' new economic awareness and perspective on the value of the dollar resembles that of a generation about 60 or 70 years their senior, the generation that lived through the Great Depression, many of whom fought or participated in World War II. The economy is faltering and the job market is bleak, forcing people to cut back on spending, save more, hunt for discounts, and use coupons. Most of our survey respondents indicated these types of changes in their behavior. In their words, they have "learned the difference between a need and a want."

Teens and young adults in particular are exercising unprecedented levels of caution. There are marketers who seem to think that, like all economic downturns of the past, the current recession will sort itself out fairly quickly and things will return to normal. It would behoove all marketers and the companies they represent to move as cautiously with this line of thinking as the Millennials are moving with their spending. What we are witnessing is a cultural shift in the way young people spend their money, primarily due to the economic downturn, but also, significantly, due to a digitized shopping process that allows young people to quickly find the best deals (a process that can rapidly decrease brand loyalty). Our survey indicates that young people are currently split on whether they will return to their previous spending habits. The smart bet is that they will not return and will instead continue to follow the cultural shift of economic awareness. They have learned to live without certain luxuries and are more cautious than ever about laying down big bucks for an item for which they can't justify the need.

Despite the fact that these teens and young adults are cautious about spending, they're still not willing to commit to a job they don't love—even after witnessing the current deep recession. The National Association of Colleges and Employers, which conducts an annual survey of thousands of recent college graduates, found that 41 percent of job seekers turned down offers in 2010. That's the same exact percentage that turned down such offers in

2007! Whether operating in a booming or recessionary economy, Millennials are just not willing to compromise their happiness for a job they don't love. Much has been written about older Millennials who feel entitled to jobs that they love, whereas their parents at times were just happy to be gainfully employed. How can you blame them, though? Members of this generation were taught that "everyone is a winner" and would often see their parents argue for a higher grade they may not have deserved. At some point, we're going to have to deal with this entitlement issue. It's making its way into offices all over the world—and shocking the heck out of boomer bosses.

Overall, interaction with Millennials is not about marketing to a demographic anymore; it's about marketing to a mind-set. In the next chapter, I break down the four predominant mind-sets of today's young people, which I call *tribes*: techies, preppies, alternatives, and independents.

> **Marketing Moment:** While Millennials are still spending plenty of money, their parents have an even bigger role in those decisions in this postrecession era. To be successful, you have to make sure there's a parental incentive to purchase, which could be as simple as a discount.

Along with the shift in mind-set about spending, Millennials are used to using technological tools to get things done faster, both when shopping and when performing everyday activities. Older generations may think that Millennials are cutting corners, but that is not often the case. The fact is that technology has found ways to improve processes and turnaround times in exponential multiples. This does not always correlate with a lower-quality product. It will be interesting to observe how Millennials, led by folks like Mark Zuckerberg and Shawn Fanning, continue to change the ways we think about human life, through methods of interacting (Facebook) and sharing (Napster). As one of our survey respondents highlighted when asked about the impact of the recessions, "Family will always be around, money won't." Even if times are tight, the human race is experiencing times of unprecedented sharing and collaboration. Millennials are in the driver's seat, and they have a better grasp of staying grounded than we give them credit for.

TINA'S TOP 5

1. Today's Millennials are more wired than any generation before them.
2. The Millennial generation includes three subsets: tweens, teens, and young adults.
3. Over 85 percent of Millennial survey respondents say their lives have been changed by the recession.
4. With Millennials, it's not about marketing to a demographic, it's about marketing to a mind-set.
5. Millennials are global mobiles, and they expect their brands to be global, too.

1. *Today's Millennials are more wired than any generation before them.* Today's youth are plugged in. They live their lives constantly checking e-mail, text messages, and browsing online with their handheld devices. This may make some of them distracted, but we're seeing the benefits of always being connected to each other. We learn a lot more about the things they are interested in, and the constant stream of communication is full of valuable data that demonstrates predictable habits and shifts in preferences. Brands will have to continue to work with younger people where they are most comfortable, on their phones and computers.

With every upside, there is a downside, and it's no different with this wired generation. Cybersafety is a very prevalent issue in today's digital landscape, one that extends to so many different areas: protection of information, actual safety concerns in regard to cyberbullying, and the psychological effects of spending so much time online. An MTV–Associated Press Study estimates

(continued)

(*continued*)

that over 50 percent of 14- to 24-year-olds have suffered some type of digital abuse.

Then there's the ongoing war between Facebook and its 500 million members. What information do users own, and what is considered private? Can there be any *true* privacy when you willingly utilize the technology provided by Facebook?

Finally, how do brands get into the game? There is so much fear associated with allowing consumers to somehow take control over a brand—something I completely understand. If you're a brand that's invested billions into an image, do you necessarily want to hand that over to Millennials? Heck, if you've even spent $5 on marketing and invested tons of sweat equity, I doubt you'd want to relinquish control. But you have to—to some extent—in order to get in the game. Technology is not going away and cannot be ignored. To reach Millennials, brands nowadays have to have to get totally wired.

2. *The Millennial generation includes three subsets: tweens, teens, and young adults.* In the next chapter, I will introduce the four "tribes" that most adequately represent the mind-sets of today's youth: techies, preppies, alternatives, and independents. However, we can learn from the numbers, so to speak, by following kids up the age ladder as they become tweens (8 to 12) and start to identify their tribes, who then develop strong individualism as teens (13 to 19), which is reflected in their spending and living habits, and who finally take the leap into adulthood as young adults (20 to 26) and start making decisions for themselves instead of relying on others for financial support.

Each subset also has its own wants, needs, and desires. Tweens aspire to be older. They seek aspiration from brands. They are still very connected to their parents and need security. Acceptance is also very important to tweens, and no matter what the brand is, they must know that their friends also like and accept that brand.

Teens are at a place in their lives where they need to feel inspired. They're becoming more independent and no longer need to feel acceptance from their friends when it comes to brands. They want to be cool, but they're doing it their own way. To get a teen's attention, you will also have to be disruptive and literally shake things up. There must always be value with this group, since there will always be something else that requires their money and time.

3. *Over 85 percent of Millennial survey respondents say their lives have been changed by the recession.* Older generations often regard young people as less aware of the economic environment and the workings of financial economy. I'd actually argue that some young people have *more* awareness than their older counterparts, as they are finding it harder than ever to find even part-time jobs, and some of them are starting their own businesses in their teens—showing that their awareness goes beyond just their shopping habits. Ironically, the Millennials could teach us all a thing or two about how to save, especially by identifying ways that technology can make certain things in life cheaper. Shopping on sites like eBay for discount goods, along with price comparison, is a compelling advantage in this sphere.

It's important for marketers to understand that there's a major shift in consumer spending presently occurring. Brands that offer 40 to 50 percent off on a regular basis cannot go back to charging full price. The consumer mentality has definitely changed—and Mom is back in the driver's seat. She's thrifty and always on the hunt for a deal, but also wants to keep her family happy. If you can figure out how to satisfy moms, it will definitely pay off in the long run.

The value proposition is no longer just a space filler on a business plan (if it ever was). It should be the first thing you consider when you're creating a new brand for Millennials.

4. *With Millennials, it's not about marketing to a demographic, it's about marketing to a mind-set.* The old days of marketing were

(continued)

(*continued*)

about pushing out a product through advertising and aiming it at a select group of individuals, usually categorized by age, gender, and sometimes ethnicity (demographic). The modern world of marketing requires much more work on the part of marketers, who now have to pull their customers toward them by directly engaging through digital means.

This is a totally new way to market products, but it's been successful for brands like Playtex Sport, for example. Playtex decided to market a product to a mind-set, sporty girls and women, not solely to a demographic, 13- to 19-year-old girls. It turned into a multibillion-dollar business. Understanding how this type of marketing can work for your brand is so successful for marketing it.

The good news is this: All of the tools needed for direct customer feedback are in place. Run a Twitter search for your product (with a #hashtag) and read some real-time reviews. Young people are telling us what they want; we just have to listen.

5. *Millennials are global mobiles, and they expect their brands to be global, too.* It wasn't so long ago that things like studying abroad or taking a trip to Asia to visit a pen pal were uncommon. Now, everyone is on the go, making the world smaller than ever. Brands and trends can go viral (and therefore global) in a matter of minutes with the right online buzz. Word of mouth literally extends to every corner of the planet, largely thanks to wireless-enabled mobile devices and more robust broadband infrastructure. Finding a target market means thinking globally and finding ways to reach potential customers across any sea and on top of any mountain.

In 1999, MTV introduced young adults to a floating university via its show *Road Rules*, which focused on Semester at Sea. From the Bahamas to Brazil to Vietnam, viewers got to see what life was like when students attended college virtually *on* the ocean. Throughout its *Real World* and *Road Rules* programs, MTV has been a pioneer in showing Millennials the world. Brands like McDonald's, Coca-Cola, and Abercrombie & Fitch are global phenomena.

Marketers must remember that even though Millennials crave global brands, they have to remain local at the same time. While this is a fine line to walk, it provides enormously valuable payoff.

Answer: True. Our survey showed that 86 percent of respondents shop online.

2

The Tribes and Their Trends

Figuring Out What Kids Want When They're More Different than Alike

Pop Quiz

If you were going to market a prepaid mobile phone to one of these tribes, which one would it be?

a. Techies
b. Preppies
c. Alternatives
d. Independents

If you enter a roomful of crying but healthy babies, chances are they all share at least one of the same needs: food, sleep, a diaper, or some undivided attention from a loving grown-up. As they grow into early childhood, they will hit the same developmental benchmarks at roughly the same time, and they'll still want and need lot of the same basics (snacks, naps, potty, hugs), though they are beginning to assert their distinct personalities. Even before preschool, the differences start to emerge. This kid loves soccer, that one only wears sandals, this kid cares about animals, this one is afraid of animals, and this kid collects menus. And so it goes as they grow, with each young soul becoming his or her own person.

Any parent or teacher will tell you that, although they may have similarities, all children are different. Yet we consistently make the mistake of behaving as if they all want and need the same things. While this is obviously practical and necessary on many levels, children become even *less* alike as they grow into their tween and teenage years—and we still often act as if they're all cut from the same cloth. This true paradox is that tweens, especially, are bursting out of their early childhood selves, trying to figure out where they fit in, attracted to and afraid of the idea of more independence. They want to be "like the other kids," but they have already formed a distinct set of likes and dislikes. They face a substantial challenge in striking a balance between being like their peers and flexing their one-of-a-kind personalities.

Marketers—and society in general—have typically categorized people by their age. You might read something like, "Adult males between the ages of 35 and 45 are more likely to have a Facebook account than adult males between the ages of . . ." or "New Yorkers between the ages of 15 and 18 are using the subway at alarming rates." Classifying people by age makes it easy to survey them and is often appropriate. However, in an era of growing individualism and the use of technological profiles to display individual characteristics, it's important to see past the demographic boundaries and begin to define people based on their cultural attributes—instead of focusing first on numbers.

While we may be inclined to think of them as "ages 9 to 12," the 12-year-old may be making the same choices as a 15-year-old, and the 9-year-old may be an early adopter of certain trends, regardless of his or her age. It's not about how we view them; it's about how they define themselves—and how the lines often blur between the tween and teenage groups. With that in mind, I've developed a new system for looking at teens and tweens by separating them into four tribes: the wired Techie; the conformist but somewhat paradoxical Preppy; the always-mellow Alternative; and the cutting-edge Independent. We'll have look at each of these in further detail, but first, it's important to explain *why* we need to look at Millennials in this way.

At some point, we began to blur the lines of which brands, products, and services should be consumed by whom. Later on, I'm going to talk in depth about the concept of a "tweenebe." *Tweenebes* are adults who want to be tweens. Now, they may not truly want to be 12 again, but they are consuming a 12-year-old's culture and loving it. Do you know those moms who love Justin Bieber? Are you one of them? Do you know dads who seem to enjoy rocking out to the Disney channel more than they should? It's okay; they're just enjoying the benefits of being a tween. I have to admit, in a society full of major economic, social, and political concerns, we'd all love to fawn over the latest tween singing sensation, read a Twilight book, or grab a Frappuccino with friends. Oh wait—don't we already do those things? I think that there are more tweenebes out there than I can even imagine.

As we look at these tribes, we have to ask ourselves: Do you have to be 13 to be a Preppy? Twenty something to be an Independent? No, you don't. That seems like an easy question to answer, but it has stumped marketers for generations. Now, I doubt that you'll see an ad for Tampax Pearl in *Sports Illustrated* or a Justin Bieber ad in *AARP* magazine, but you will see major brand extensions happening over the next few years. And I'm not talking about product development; I'm talking about market development. Marketers have to get outside of thinking in boxes, whether it's ages 7 to 12, 13 to 19, or 20 to 24.

Technology has created so many generationally shared experiences. Facebook is no longer for elite college students. Indeed, the fastest growing demographic on Facebook is women over 50. How people think, feel, and react to brands is a completely new experience. Because of that, I've developed four tribes that I feel are universal. I think that these tribes definitely have subtribes (to be explored in another book at some point), and I do believe that consumers can belong to more than one tribe. But the tribal migration is happening, and has been happening for years. As with any good disruptive innovation, technology has forced us to deal with this issue.

Ten years ago, if you wanted to launch a new product for teens, you'd probably launch a major ad campaign in a teen magazine like *Seventeen*. You would likely reach more than 10 million girls and call it a day. Fast-forward to 2010, where readership of *Seventeen* is now about 4 million. Where did all those readers go? Well, they're online, of course. They're on thousands of web sites. How are you going to find them? Well, sure, you can just launch a campaign on a network of web sites and hope that you're going to reach your entire target.

However, there's an easier way. Targeting a tribe is also about understanding a mind-set. A *tribe* is defined as a "social division of people." The key word here is *social*. Social involves so many things. What are people doing? How are they doing it? With whom are they doing it? How often? How long? When? Where? This is starting to sound like an invitation to the best party. That's the mind-set a marketer should have when thinking about tribes, and that's why tribal marketing works.

If you start to think about these consumers—Preppies, Techies, Alternatives, and Independents—as tribes, and then think about all of their social activities, you can easily figure out how to reach them. Then you won't just be bowling in the dark. You will hit your mark every time.

Now you're ready to get to know these tribes.

The Wired Techie

Philip is always the first of his friends to know about a new technology. In fact, he usually buys one and sells another before most people even know it exists. He is the guy asking you questions like, "How much RAM do you have?" or "Which generation is your phone?" Getting in touch with Philip is never a problem. He always has a connection up and running, be it through Skype video calls, mobile devices loaded with AIM and Twitter apps, Facebook, or just good old e-mail.

Philip aspires to be involved in the creative/entertainment industry, and he is incredibly passionate about new technology. He buys new gadgets on impulse and often discards them before they are adopted by the mainstream. He finds freedom, organization, simplicity, and connectivity in technology and is proud of his technical acumen.

Philip is the Techie of the Millennial generation.

Without a doubt, these wired youth are setting the tone and the pace for the rest of the world. Techies have a great sense of what's practical and possible with technology and are creative enough to put their ideas to good use.

Techies used to be called *nerds* in prior generations. Movies like *The Breakfast Club* and *Revenge of the Nerds* series painted pictures of these individuals as societal outcasts who were picked on and never accepted in the popular peer groups. They kept to themselves, aced all of their classes, and played video and computer games endlessly. It seems that *Revenge of the Nerds* had it right, because nerds have developed into Techies who are now popular, have sex appeal, and start companies overnight.

The reason for this newfound mainstream popularity is simple: Techies know the most about how modern things work. As technology pervades every corner of everyday life and machines continue to substitute humans, Techies are irreplaceable. Their advice is highly sought after, and they then dictate to their peers what's cool and what's not. Technology is the new fashion, and Techies have become the trendsetters.

Think about it: Everyone has a personal computer and a mobile device. It's fairly impossible to finish a conversation these days without someone whipping out an iPhone to look up something in Wikipedia or to show off a new app that makes buying movie tickets easier. Techies dominate these conversations, because they usually know how to execute tasks more quickly—and may have even developed the app themselves. Because they understand the underpinnings of how all of these devices and applications are connected, they are constantly coming up with new ideas to make life easier. Their dreams involve wireless technology that will connect every corner of the globe, and they're working toward that end constantly.

Not only have Techies started to join the popular crowd; they're using their knowledge of technology to launch some extremely lucrative companies and ideas. For example, the founder of Foursquare, Naveen Selvadurai, recently raised $20 million and has attracted 2 million users to his geolocator. Not too shabby for a Techie. Whereas in the past, the jocks and the Preppies (more on them later) used to attract the most attention—and seemed pointed toward the most attractive and profitable career paths—Techies are now the front-runners to gain fame and notoriety. They frequently even manage to do this without ever attending (or at least graduating from) college.

Now that we know who the Techies are, we have to ask: What do they want? Techies absolutely *must* to be the first people to try new devices and gadgets. As far as they're concerned, this isn't a want; it's a *need*. If you are developing a new tech product, it is of utmost importance that you attract and find these Techies.

Why are they so important? Well, first of all, they can offer valuable feedback during crucial development stages. How they interact with your technology is a big indicator of how other groups, like Preppies, might engage with the product as well. Techies, by way of definition, are also going to be the ones to introduce your new technology to their friends. In some cases, they might even have to explain it, set it up on their friends' smartphones, and give them a quick tutorial.

Besides being the first to actually try new tools, Techies also like to be on top of their emergence and always aware of what's coming next. Web sites like Gizmodo.com, which has more than 6.2 million monthly visitors, are the first stop for today's Techies, as well as for Millennial Techies, and 70 percent of Gizmodo.com's audience is between the ages of 18 and 34.

Techies also want to use their specialized skills to interact with other tribes, especially Preppies. Gone are the days of images of nerds congregating among themselves. Techies want to teach their peers how to interact with technology and gadgets, which is one reason they make great brand ambassadors and evangelists for new products. Who better to introduce a new gadget or tool than a Techie?

Techies also need to invest in functional products that streamline their lives, which is why they adapted to Foursquare, Twitter, and Facebook so quickly. Sure, the other tribes have to buy in to create global phenomena, but it all starts with the Techies. They are always looking for disruptive innovation.

Finally, Techies *need* to value innovation and the future. It's in their DNA. These things matter above all—even price—to the Techie. Funnily enough, this extends to other tribes as well. In our recent Buzz Marketing Group Recession Study, we found that all respondents were more likely to give up clothing, dining out, and shoes before they'd give up their electronics. These gadgets are the new fashion.

If your target is the Techie, you must remember that Techies embrace brands that respect their knowledge, challenge their skills, and provide them with a cutting-edge, high-quality product.

The Conformist Yet Somewhat Paradoxical Preppy

Greg is a perfect example of the preppy, "on-the-surface," sometimes paradoxical member of the majority. Don't let his name-brand clothes fool you into thinking he is as simple as the football jock who just wants to party. He does use his wardrobe to fit in with the masses, since he doesn't feel the need to dress too weirdly or attempt to creatively become America's next fashion icon. However, his intelligence and ambition contradicts some of the stereotypes often associated with Preppies. He has the unique ability to fit in with the majority, yet he is truly more complicated than he sometimes lets on.

On the outside, Greg seems like the all-American boy with a huge smile who's a pleasure to be around. But if you dig deeper, you'll find that he loves to learn about new subjects and never strays too far from his guitar. There could be some musical aspirations that are trying to poke through his mainstream exterior.

Greg is the Preppy of the Millennial generation.

Preppies may be the most identifiable tribe in sight, but marketing to them is not as easy as you think. They want to fit in, and the easiest way to do so is to look the part. This tribe clamors for the attention of their peers and considers themselves the popular crowd. From a fashion standpoint, they are traditional (Gap) yet trendy (J. Crew). They stick to brand names, and they are often confused with the mannequins seen in the store windows where they shop. In other words, they're not going to be the tribe that takes many chances, as they are far more focused on keeping up with popular trends and sticking with the "in crowd." In this sense, Preppies are the megaphones—the ones marketers want to infect with their "virus." They can cause a tremor to become a full-blown trend.

Preppies tend to choose more traditional careers, such as finance and law, often due to their parents' (who may have followed similar paths) choices and influence. But as the traditional industries continue to shrink and the suit-and-tie crowd is being forced into alternative professions or entrepreneurial life, Preppies are going to have to make some adjustments. Though their fashion sense and social circles may not change, we may see Preppies start to explore other ways of life, as the mainstream career choices begin to fragment.

By analyzing Preppy career choices, we can see that Preppies tend to shift gears a few years after they've conformed. Older preppies are known to rebel, perhaps because they spent so much of their youth swimming laps in the mainstream. This makes sense when we consider that conventional approaches will always exist and can get boring for some. While others will continue to follow along the well-trodden path, you must always keep an eye out for those who may be ready to start incorporating another tribe's characteristics.

What do Preppies want and need in a brand experience? Their major desire is to feel like part of a group or a movement. It's interesting, however, that Preppies aren't usually the ones to start the movement. While it may sound strange, we all know a few so-called Preppies in our lives. Maybe it's the parent who is passionate about issues at her child's school; although she might not run for PTA president, she's present at all of the meetings. Or perhaps it's the soccer player everyone loves who, though not the team captain, is always raising the most money for team fund-raisers. The bottom line is that, while they may not always be change agents, Preppies will always be game changers.

Preppies are the megaphones that bring your message to the masses. Their need to feel like part of a group or movement propels them to be effective communicators. That's what you need if your brand or product is going to succeed.

Preppies want to be trendy; style matters to this group. While high-quality, streamlined technology may be all you need for Techies, if you really want to reach that magical tipping point, you need to do it with style and trendiness. The case study presented later in this chapter is an example of what happens when we ignore major trends in favor of focusing solely on good service.

Preppies also want to be liked. That's why you can find them in obvious places like sports teams, social clubs, fraternity and sorority houses, or volunteer organizations—and why they are usually among the most-liked people there. Preppies are the ones who have thousands of Facebook friends, who want and need to be liked. This is another reason they make such good consumers. You know that ad with the guy who's dressed in those great pants and who has all of those beautiful girls following him? That *matters* to Preppy guys. They might tell you in a focus group that it means nothing to see the Old Spice guy in a commercial, but sales say something totally different. Likability matters.

Preppies need to conform, to obey the rules, to play the game. They want the expected outcome. How else could *Cosmopolitan* sell millions of magazines to Preppy young women each month? These readers truly believe that following those cover story tips will land them that perfect guy, perfect wardrobe, and perfect body. It's the same for Preppy teens, as well. That new Cover Girl mascara? They're hoping its application will quickly convert to three dates by week's end.

There is definitely a "do this and you'll get that" formula at play with Preppies. In order to resonate with them, that value proposition needs to be very clear to them, even if it's not written in black and white. If you ask most young women why they're investing money in certain beauty brands, it's not because they *need* to wear mascara; after all, their lashes won't fall off without it! It's because of how it makes them feel, and because they expect a certain outcome from that brand experience.

Preppies do not want to go against the grain, which is a very important delineation between them and other tribes. You'll find out later that this is not necessarily true with the other tribes, who love to start revolutions. Preppies aren't going to take the heat for trying something new—because, again, they want an expected outcome. Some might see this as being calculating, but I consider them very good brand managers. They have a personal brand, and they know what their values are. They're not willing to lose cool points by going against the grain.

What's a marketer to do? I believe that Preppies embrace brands that provide them with the necessary tools to make them feel as though they are trendy, part of the group, and fitting into the social norms. Plenty of brands offer that: J. Crew, Cover Girl, Hollister, and Coca-Cola, to name just a few.

Verizon Wireless: FREEUP to FREE DONE

In 2002, mobile carrier Verizon Wireless launched [FREEUP], a pay-as-you-go service for teens. The launch release stated, "Stylish teens from coast-to-coast can now [FREEUP] with

(continued)

(*continued*)

Get It NowSM prepay service and download applications to the newest Verizon Wireless prepay color phone offering—the T720PP by Motorola."[1] The service seemed interesting enough: It offered Verizon's award-winning network, tons of freebies and add-ons, and a free phone. This seemed like the perfect scenario for a youthful brand.

An ad agency hired my firm to conduct research with consumers about brand creativity. While the premise of our research was that cool kids, or Preppies, wanted a prepaid service, I argued that they didn't. I went even further by suggesting that Techies, who at this time were still considered geeks, were the true targets for this initiative. It was 2002, and the geeks just weren't cool enough yet.

Though little is known about [FREEUP]'s demise, it seems an alternative brand got the positioning right—and did so light-years ahead of the competition. Later that year, Virgin Mobile introduced a prepaid brand that targeted teens. The company's hook: a brand-new Matrix 3 phone. Eight years later, Virgin Mobile is still selling prepaid plans. Its latest campaign: "After years of stupid cell phone plans, here's a crazy one—$25/Month." For that fee, users get unlimited messaging, e-mail, data, Web, and 300 minutes. The ad ends with the tagline: "Don't be stupid, go crazy."

What did Verizon miss eight years ago? Well, prepaid phones simply weren't cool. Verizon focused so heavily on the plans, what you could do, and its great network . . . but never on the actual phone. Virgin Mobile launched its program with the Matrix 3 phone—the coolest, trendiest device around—and found instant success. Virgin Mobile realized that Preppies need to feel stylish and trendy, and they need their phones to be stylish and trendy, too. Let this be a lesson to any brand that feels that its service offerings are enough to attract Millennials. It's not just about the service you offer; it's about providing the "cool factor" to customers who greatly care about such things.

The Always Mellow Alternative

Laura is the definition of mellow. She might seem simple and easygoing at first glance, but a longer, deeper look sheds light on her creativity and style. She is the kind of girl who can hang out with the trendiest social groups and also hang out with the outcasts, nerds, and Preppies. She finds satisfaction in expressing herself and in being creative and innovative. This allows her the freedom to flow from group to group while maintaining her mellow, down-to-earth, likable personality.

Laura keeps an open mind when meeting new people and exploring what makes them tick. She likes to know the motivations behind others' actions and wants to be around people who have a passion for their pursuits. Although you'll never catch her without a camera, she doesn't use it to take party pics with her friends. Instead, Laura is always looking for a new way to capture the essence of life around her in both people and nature. She has an undeniable kindness and compassion for the planet and its inhabitants.

Laura is the Alternative of the Millennial generation.

Simply put, the Alternatives are the future. Their laid-back and go-with-the-flow nature allows them to effortlessly incorporate trends and ideas into their lifestyles. This makes them frequent early adopters who are completely willing and eager to try new things. They have no fear of not fitting in; in fact, they find fitting in stressful. They hate conformity and crave independence.

As the world continues to fragment and traditional ways of living and doing business dissolve further, Alternatives may be the tribe best suited to make the quickest impact once they reach the age of maturity. For example, Alternatives started the ecologically conscious Green trend years before anyone else saw the need for it. They value the environment and survival of the planet very highly, something that's reflected in their preferences across the board—from their fashion choices to the types of products they purchase. They read and talk about their favorite causes *a lot*. Once they decide to do something about it, they find ways to get going quickly by doing research online and participating in volunteer groups to make sure that their voices are being heard.

Culturally, Alternatives are likely to be less concerned with others' opinions and making a lot of money than with taking humanitarian trips to the third world to help the impoverished. As they get older, they will live and breathe for their causes and disregard societal pressures to live a more traditional lifestyle.

This tribe should always be the center of attention for marketers. While Alternatives will buy products and services that are available to the mainstream, they often use them in ways that the producers may not have intended. Their passion for doing good works in the world and caring for the planet define the messages that companies now seek to include in their advertising and marketing campaigns. Alternatives will be very valuable in the coming years, as Green initiatives continue to explode. They have a lot of insight to offer regarding what types of environmental campaigns are most effective.

Members of this group are also very likely to start their own companies and/or nonprofits (to tackle tricky humanitarian issues). These are the happy-go-lucky kids whom the *New York Times* dubbed "The Why-Worry Generation." With an unemployment rate close to 20 percent for 20-to 24-year-olds, you would think that they'd snap up any job offered to them. However, as I said earlier, 41 percent of these Millennial job seekers turned down offers in 2010. Why would they do that? Well, Alternatives have different values, and these values definitely influence other tribes.

Alternatives need to maintain a sense of independence. This is a very important value for them. Who they are and what they believe is not something they figure out as a member of a group; it's something that they must determine independently, on their own journey. Once they've deciphered exactly who and what this is, they'll engage with brands that meet that definition. Sounds a lot like young adults who crave reflection and self-fulfillment from brands, right? Yes, Alternatives are a driving force behind that philosophy.

Alternatives want to be on the cusp of the more off-the-wall, nontraditional events. This is why brands that enlist the help of guerilla marketing seem to play well to this tribe. Whether it's an unannounced live event that pops up on a college campus, a Save Darfur rally, or a one-day flea market, Alternatives don't want to feel as though they're missing out on something that is not the norm.

It's also no secret that Alternatives are passionate about music. This satisfies their need to feel connected, which makes sense. What other avenue seems more important to maintaining your true self and having an amazing, off-the-wall experience than attending an indie rock concert? It could be a campus band or unknowns at the local hang out, but whatever the performance or venue, Alternatives use their passion for music to see themselves in the artists they support.

Alternatives also like to be relaxed and not stressed out. If there is a rush to do something or be somewhere that doesn't connect with their alternative culture, then you really won't find them there. They like to take the time to figure out what brands they relate to most, without having messaging crammed down their throats. If you're really trying to reach an alternative, it may have to be done through a brand or a cause they're already committed to.

Alternatives also crave a creative outlet. It isn't necessarily making music, although many alternatives do. It could be through photography, fashion design, or writing, but they need to be creative. Giving them the tools to be creative is a great way to connect with this tribe. Whether it's sponsoring a competition or allowing Alternatives to help develop a campaign or initiative, they will love the opportunity to be creative.

Alternatives need brands that respect their space and allow them to adapt products to their own individual use, without forcing them to sacrifice their individuality or compromise their values. This is a tightrope to walk, but when Alternatives are into your brand or service, they can compel other tribes to pay attention as well. Just think of what effect they've had on the Green movement, both culturally and financially. That's a significant impact.

The Cutting-Edge Independent

Harry is a true trendsetter in every sense of the word. He walks to the beat of his own drum and embraces diversity and change. As a young artist, he beams with confidence and is an established leader in his social networks. He identifies himself as a creator, spoken-word poet, friend and mentor, and entrepreneur. He's unafraid of the unknown and prefers to find his own way. He describes a 9 to 5 job as "slavery."

Harry believes that conforming is impossible to avoid, so he chooses to always "conform to nonconformity." Although it happens anyway, he doesn't set out to have others follow him; he'd much rather inspire people to search for their own individuality.

Harry is the Independent of the Millennial generation.

While Alternatives deviate from the mainstream in order to stay true to their causes, Independents deviate for the sake of deviating. It's as if this tribe understands that if they dig deep enough and read between the lines, they will always find something worthwhile.

Part of what drives Independents' decisions is that they aren't afraid to support the little guy. In fact, they thrive by championing not-yet-popular brands and ways of life. In this respect, Independents are the lifeblood of start-ups and small businesses. They focus on market newcomers' cultural impact and provide unabashed support of new cutting-edge concepts. Independents spend as much time researching the newest exclusive limited editions of clothing, music, and tech gadgets as they do buying them.

However, Independents' attention tends to wane substantially once a brand or concept finds mainstream appeal. This inclination allows them to remain independent and quickly move on to the next little guy, hoping to uncover another gem as yet undiscovered by the masses. For example, Independents with a sneaker obsession will likely have various resources for shopping for exclusive, limited-edition shoes that are not found in the neighborhood Foot Locker. Instead, they turn to various underground web sites, local and regional wholesalers, and various intermediaries on the sneaker food chain. They use other trusted independents' word-of-mouth advice to find what they are looking for: the pair of sneakers that no one else has. When they get to school the next day, they are looking for one reaction: "Where did you get *those*? I haven't seen them before." This statement alone makes all of the searching worthwhile to Independents. However, as soon as a few others start to wear the same pair of sneakers, Independents tuck their shoes away in the closet and are back on the hunt for the next undiscovered pair.

Fashion, in particular, is experiencing an influx of Independents ruling the ranks at fashion shows. Up-and-coming fashion design trendsetters like Bianca and Coco Brandolini d'Adda, Gaia Repossi, Shala Monroque, Alexa Chung, and Eugenie Niarchos are commonly seen sitting in the front row at some of the world's biggest fashion shows, displaying to the world that independent thinkers and tastemakers are guiding the direction of new styles. In fact, their presence as the new establishment is setting the tone for young people to be more heavily involved in creating and marketing their own designs.

All in all, the Independents crave new things, not shiny ones. They dare to be different, and they like to help brands break into the mainstream just so they can abandon them and find the next big thing. They are dollar-conscious, looking for the biggest bang for their buck instead of focusing on more expensive name brands, and they thrive in indie environments that feel cozy, seem exclusive, and foster brainstorming and creativity.

Independents need to be autonomous, passionate thinkers. Passion is key. How many times have we heard that someone has a "passion for fashion" and cringed at the very thought? Yet we can't deny the impact of fashion on every area of branding and consumerism. As is true for most people, and even truer for Millennials, they define themselves by what they wear. That is the first impression you have of who they are—and for Independents, fashion is an extension of their passion.

Independents also have a need to stay in touch with their true selves. Independents won't be the ones getting caught up in Cover Girl's latest endeavor. This doesn't mean that they don't appreciate cosmetics or want to look good. They just won't allow someone to tell them how to define themselves. Unlike Preppies, they're not looking for a magic formula with a suspected outcome. The journey to discovering a new cosmetics brand or a new hip hangout is just as much about the brand as it is about them defining who they are along the way.

Independents also need to receive value for the money they spend. There are always two types of value at play: *intrinsic* and *extrinsic*. Intrinsically, it matters how the brand makes them feel. Are they buying a bag from an organization that is committed to helping women in Africa? Well, they believe in helping women, so they believe in that brand. Extrinsically, others will see it, and it will make them seem cooler to those people as well. Now, I know you're thinking, "I thought you said Independents aren't concerned with pleasing others." That truly isn't their main concern. They don't need praise from the masses. But they are part of a tribe, just as the others are, and it matters how those other members feel about them and their values.

Independents want and need to make a statement. Self-expression is important to Millennials as a whole, but when it comes to Alternatives and Independents, it's a major priority. Every day, in every way they can, they want to make a statement about who they are and what they believe. These two tribes share many common values, even if they have different motivators. It's important for marketers to consider the interconnectivity of these tribes. Brands that make big statements are really attractive to Independents. I believe that in the Millennial generation, the majority of Independents are found in the older teen and young adult subsets.

Independents need to feel that their thoughts and feelings are heard. This definitely involves political statements. Young people care deeply about politics, not just on a national level, on a global level as well. Independents were a key tribe for President Obama in the 2008 election. They were into him before it became status quo to root for him. They attached to his thoughts and ideals, which they shared. Independents are important to politics. They're not like Preppies, who wait for a critical mass. If you can snag Independents from the start, they will be loyal to your cause and bring many other people with them.

Independents embrace brands and products that reflect their rebellious, selective nature while providing them with value for their money. That's a lot to accomplish, but if you can do it, you will have an incredibly loyal customer.

Marketing Moment: Don't be afraid to step away from tradition. Millennials think and live in a totally different way than previous generations. You have to understand their mind-set to understand them. And you must realize that in some instances, a 12-year-old and a 16-year-old may actually want the same thing.

The Buzzword Is . . . *Instanity*

One trend that all four tribes and their various offshoots experience is something that I call "instanity"—the idea that, regardless of our age, we all live in this insanity of "now!" We need instant results, instant action, and instant gratification. Millennials didn't pioneer this concept—that was our doing, with some assistance from previous generations. To a certain extent, it's just the American way. But today's kids may take it to a whole new level.

It started out innocently enough. Don't wait to see the photos you just snapped; they're instantly displayed on your camera. Why wait 15 hours to watch the Australian Open on TV when results are streaming live on the Internet (with highlights posted hourly on YouTube)? Need to call your sister or check your bank balance? Do it *right now* on that smartphone of yours while you're in line to see the movie that you can't wait for on DVD. (Whoops, you're not *in* line because you bought your advance tickets *on*line.) Want to read my book after it's published? Amazon says that you can start reading the book of your choice in under a minute (is that fast enough?), when you download it onto your Kindle. (Don't have a Kindle? You can have it tomorrow if you order it in the next four hours and 37 minutes and choose one-day shipping!) *Instanity* is about our addiction to an increased need for speed combined with an insatiable urge to multitask.

What does that mean for marketers? Well, operating in a world of instanity can be a dangerous thing. There is no time for careful examination, and sometimes the results can be extremely detrimental. Take, for example, the firing of Shirley Sherrod, who lost her job at the United States Department of Agriculture (USDA) over false racism allegations. Sherrod was forced to resign after blogger Andrew Brietbart posted (on his web site) selective clips of a speech she had given at an NAACP event. The first news outlet to respond to this posting was Foxnews.com. Many others quickly followed suit, thus legitimizing this video. As mass hysteria erupted on the blogosphere, Sherrod was forced to resign. After her resignation, the NAACP put out a statement saying her statements were appalling. Sherrod continued to defend herself, claiming she was forced to resign by an administration that was "fearful of Fox News and the Tea Party." What happened over the next 24 hours was unbelievable. Every news network, the NAACP, and even the White House had to retract their criticisms of Sherrod. It was a public embarrassment of epic proportions, and it's a great example of the instanity that's taken over the media. It no longer matters whether a story is true, it matters who tells it first. And networks wonder why viewership is down? If viewers want speculation and gossip, they'll go to gossip news networks and blogs. When they come to trusted sources like Fox and CNN, they're coming for news—vetted news.

This example doesn't even center on Millennials. Rather, it's a case of veteran newscasters being victims of instanity. Had just one person taken the time to investigate this story for even a few more hours, Sherrod may have kept her job. It also could have spared the White House, not to mention all the news networks, a substantial amount of embarrassment.

Yet shockingly, the feedback in this situation included answers like, "Well, what were we supposed to do?" And excuses such as, "The news cycle never stops." This is all true, but we have to be responsible for the choices we make. What does this say to Millennials? That it's okay to be caught up in the instanity of now—just as long as we apologize later? This trend is destroying our culture. It's not about the need to be connected online, and it's not about being afraid of the future. It's about the effects of living life so instantly, so "in the moment," that we neglect to consider the potential repercussions of our actions and leave a path of destruction behind us. Consider that sometimes, Millennials (or any other generation, for that matter) may not be able to repair the damage they've done.

Although it's nice to get those shoes delivered via same-day service, we might want to consider vetting other, more important issues. After all, true innovation requires time to make impactful changes. Without that time, we're left with a lot of noise and a bunch of half-finished projects, concepts, and ideas.

TINA'S TOP 5

1. *We can no longer market to Millennials based on their age alone. Their mind-set is the most powerful way to reach them.* Separating tweens and teens into tribes is a new method for looking at young people's habits instead of clustering them into groups based on age. Studying the ways that they think allows us to garner results that transcend age and, quite often, gender as well. Although the four tribes I describe may not be completely and mutually exclusive of each other, they provide a great starting point for marketers; they delve into these young people's thought processes, focusing in particular on the ways that they try to distinguish themselves from one another. Even mainstream-minded Preppies are providing clues about how they want to be identified: They may not be the ones to break out the latest trends, but they offer key indicators about which brands will have a lasting impact and which ones will be around for only a season or two.

2. *Tribal marketing will make you more effective.* When hoping to launch a new product, marketers can use the tribal system to identify which groups of young people will be the most likely to be early adopters, late adopters, and viral leaders. This provides a pyramid system from which to gauge the progress of a brand and its products.

Once you identify your tribe, it's critical that you educate yourself on the things of utmost importance to them. Do they need to feel like part of a group? Do they need to be the first to try new technology? Is maintaining independence the most critical thing? Must they stay in touch with their true selves? You have to identify motivators, then create plans based on those major concepts and trends.

3. *Millennials can have a primary tribe and a secondary one.* Although it's important to identify a young person's tribe—and, accordingly, what this indicates about their thought processes

(continued)

(*continued*)

and lifestyle habits—it's vital to remember that most young people are complex and will have different tribal layers to consider. For example, a hard-core Techie who is an ace with the latest electronic trends and is already dabbling in software coding may also be extremely passionate about independent rock music and decide to develop software apps to try to create gateways for new music to be heard. The same could be true for an eco-friendly Preppy who supports name brands but will shop only for those that embrace cause-based marketing and use recycled products. While these four primary tribal groups are usually the easiest indicators to start with, young people, like all humans, are becoming increasingly complex: They have layers to their tastes and ambitious, just as the rest of us do.

4. *No matter what your product or service, focus on the tribe that will be your early adopter.* The others will follow. For example, Virgin Mobile focused on Techies when launching a prepaid service. Techies were the early adopters who brought in the larger tribe—conformist but somewhat paradoxical Preppies.

Launching and sustaining brands is an area in which the tribal system really helps marketers and businesses take off. The key is to get your message and product into the hands of the tribe that will be the most enthusiastic about introducing it to the marketplace. It's always critical to identify your tribe first, and then figure out what motivates them to buy. Here's a quick recap of the tribes and their early-adoptive habits:

- *Techies*. Techies will almost always be the entry point for new technical devices, mobile applications, and Web-based businesses. They understand how things work and are able to quickly articulate the pragmatic uses of technological innovations that, at first, may seem complicated to others.
- *Preppies*. Preppies are hardly ever early adopters; however, they are the engines that allow brands to scale. Marketers must aspire to have Preppies ready for the handoff as soon as the early adopters are finished launching and refining a brand at its inception.

- *Alternatives.* Alternatives are the new-wave hippies. They are constantly looking at the world's living habits and coming up with ways to do things in ways that are cleaner, safer, and more energy-efficient. They often reject the advertising of big brands unless they are putting a lot of time and effort (i.e., energy) into cause marketing, Green initiatives, and humanitarian projects.

- *Independents.* Independents are the early adopters of both fashion and entertainment that is still in the background (although it may be thriving in the underground scene). They read blogs rather than mainstream media and pay very close attention to the word of mouth spread by their friends—not only to seek new and impending ideas and trends, but also to stay away from brands and fashions that have entered the mainstream. Remember that while Independents may help you launch your brand, they won't see it through to massive scale.

It's not always easy to identify your tribe. Remember that most young people have primary and secondary tribes and that they may frequently cross the lines between them, especially as tweens grow to teens and continue to explore their interests and styles. Dig deep to find out which tribe(s) they are leaning toward, and focus your efforts accordingly.

5. *In addition, always remember the power of instanity.* Yes, there are many good elements, but it's the bad ones that we remember most! All things are cyclical, and there will come a time when we will return to a slower pace. It may not be the way our parents' generation lived or did things, but I believe that Millennials will find a way to solve this problem. Our current culture may be fast-paced, but it's important to remember that well after our time has passed, our culture will survive to tell our story.

Answer: A. But this wasn't the case in 2000. Techies were still considered nerds back then. My, how times have changed! Geek chic is everywhere.

Part Two

What Millennials Want Now

3

"I Want It"

What Millennials Buy and Why

BUZZSPOTTER PROFILE

It was 11:58. Lucy sat expectantly at her desk, watching the clock on her computer. At exactly 12 noon, she logged into her account on Gilt.com. "Yes!," she yelled—a little too loudly.

"Everything okay?" a coworker asked.

"Oh, yeah, yeah, I'm fine," she replied. But Lucy was better than fine. That superpricey Marc Jacobs bag she'd had her eye on for months just went on sale—60 percent off! She pulled out her AmEx and bought it immediately (every good Gilt shopper knows you buy now or not at all). By Friday (courtesy of expedited delivery), Lucy would be rocking the bag of her dreams. You gotta love lunch hour.

 Pop Quiz

This time, we're going to start with the answers. Here they are: Starbuck's, iPods, school lunches, Nikes, iTunes, cell phones, video games, really good cleats.

So, what was the question? Well, those are some of the responses we received when we asked our tween panelists what items they'd given up during the recession—responses that are a spot-on reflection of how tween Millennials spend much of their disposable income. From those in the older range of the age spectrum, we heard increasingly adult-sounding answers like "Eating out," "Premium cable," and, "I've had to sell my car and resort to taking the bus to school again." The sacrificed items suggest that most young people have a limited amount of disposable income, don't have credit cards, and rely on their parents or other adults for major expenses, even if they have part-time jobs. But for the most part, tweens still have a lot of disposable income to spend. While they might not be buying pricey electronics, that doesn't mean that they're not picking up their favorite beverage, grabbing a book, or buying clothes. People are still making money from tweens—and you could be one of them!

Despite these constraints, however, the kids who grew up spending less time being pushed around in grocery carts and more time on the lap of a parent browsing for deals on eBay still wield a lot of influence over where the money goes in the American marketplace. Economists estimate that the tween market accounts for billions of dollars spent in categories ranging from apparel and beauty products to candy, snacks, and beverages, electronics, toys, and entertainment. While it's hard to pinpoint an exact number ($43 billion is the estimate used by many industry professionals), we know that tweens have power. Later in this chapter, we'll take a look at where they're spending their money and what you can do to become relevant to tweens and their parents.

Many of us jump on the fact that this is a growing billion-dollar market and assume that Millennials are perhaps the most brand-conscious, materialistic, and spendthrift generation in history. We believe that they make it a top priority to have the latest style of everything—whether sneakers or a cell phones—and consider cost (or carbon footprint) to be a negligible factor. I will agree that kids today are very brand- and cost-savvy, largely because the Internet gives them unprecedented access to products and prices. But I don't think we should assume that their brand loyalty is impenetrable or that they don't care about where their money goes.

How big is this tween market, and exactly what do we need to know about it? The U.S. Census Bureau projects that there will be more than 21 million tweens in the United States by 2015, 40 percent of whom will be minorities. Our tweens are growing up in a culturally rich and diverse America, and marketers will have to respond to that. It seems that Millennials, and especially tweens, choose their groups of friends based on socioeconomic and psychological reasons—not because of race. They reason that if they go to the same school and like the same things, well then, of course they should be friends! They've been raised in a world that's focused on celebrating differences. They expect to see not only themselves when observing images from brands, but also their friends.

In the first chapter, I covered the notion of tweens' three major needs: aspiration, security, and acceptance. This concept also translates to the images they want to see. They feel secure when the pictures and advertisements for brands they love reflect a cooler version of themselves and their friends. Multicultural ad campaigns should be the norm when it comes to marketing to this generation. Diversity matters very much to them. Justice, the tween girl clothing retailer, does a very good job with its imaging.

The entertainment world seems to understand this. Some of tweens' favorite stars these days are ethnic celebrities like Beyonce, Jessica Alba, Selena Gomez, Rihanna, and even Jennifer Lopez, who is still hot with tweens (and will be even hotter, thanks to her recently appointed role as an *American Idol* judge). Tweens are seeing images of beauty from all different ethnicities everywhere—not just in content geared toward them. Actresses like Freida Pinto, Dania Ramirez, and Cameron Diaz (who often speaks proudly of her Hispanic heritage) still top hot lists.

You will see that this is true for teens, as well. In a recent Buzz Marketing Group survey, artists Drake, Lil Wayne, Black Eyed Peas, and Beyonce were all in the top 10 responses when teens were asked to name their favorite recording artists—in the company of Lady Gaga, Eminem, and Taylor Swift. Not only are they embracing diversity in imaging, they're also doing so with genre style!

Now that you know that diversity matters, you should probably determine whether your messaging fits in to the life of a busy tween. According to NPD Group's "Kid Leisure Time II," children between the ages of 5 and 12 have 58 hours of leisure time each week. Doing homework, followed by using the computer and listening to music are their favorite leisure activities.

We know that tweens are multitaskers who can pay attention to multiple screens at once. C&R research says that tweens are more likely to be doing something else while watching TV, such as homework (53 percent) or surfing online (50 percent). When you take a moment and think about the tweens you may know in your life (your children, students, nieces and nephews, etc.), you can see how this is true. Marketers have to find a way to become part of tweens' "multiple-screen" existence.

Where do you go to do this? Online. While this might seem like common sense, too many brands are resisting true online integration—despite the fact that there are so many potential destinations. Second Life is a bit dated, but sites like HabboHotel.com, which predates Facebook and MySpace, Stardoll.com, and Zwinky.com have hundreds of millions of international tween and teen members. The average Habbo user is on the site for 41 minutes per day.

Just what are they doing on sites like these? Well, they're buying virtual goods and meeting friends. Tweens crave security and acceptance—and, while most adults assume that the online world is not secure, we have to remember that tweens have lived all of their lives with this kind of technology. They don't share the fear we adults have. To them, the Internet is a safe place that we just don't get, a place where they can meet new friends who have the same interests as they do, a place to feel accepted. Maybe they're passionate about the Twilight book series, so they join a community of Twilight fans, or *Twihards*, as they're known. These networks allow them the opportunity to really interact with brands, which is exactly why brands shouldn't be timid about embracing this medium.

It can translate to offline partnerships as well. Stardoll and Burger King partnered on a fall 2010 promotion, in which the Burger King kids' meals included a real Stardoll interactive plastic "paper doll" maker.

Spotlight: Stardoll.com

Stardoll.com is the world's largest online fashion and games community for girls. Launched in 2004 as Paperdollheaven .com, the site now has more than 28 million registered users, of which 92.2 percent are female. It also has the highest concentration of tween and teen girls among the top 1,000 properties in the United States. This site is about fame, fashion, and friends for girls. Thousands of international movie and TV stars, singers, and athletes have created their own virtual paper dolls, which girls may use as their own image on the site. Celebrities like Avril Lavigne, Eve, and Justin Bieber all have lifelike images on the site. Members can also become "famous" on the site if they can win the site's Cover Girl contest. The site is also about fashion and allows users to design their own items or purchase virtual goods from well-known brands, which they can buy at StarPlaza. There are also more than 1 million clubs that girls can join. And advertisers seem to love this site as much as teen and tween girls do. Stardoll brand partners include Procter & Gamble, DKNY, and T-Mobile.

In my opinion, all campaigns for tweens should begin online. Whether we like it or not, this is where they are. While we absolutely need to include offline engagement, we must begin where they begin. Even when they're watching TV, they're still interacting online, discussing the show with their friends, surfing the Web, and listening to music.

The key is to realize there is no single thing you can do to reach tweens. To cut through the noise of their everyday lives, you have to do as many things as you can afford to do and be every place you can afford to be. And don't ever forget about the power of the parents in the decision-making process, because they hold the key (and in many cases, the purse strings!).

One thing you need to keep in mind is that *tweens love marketing.* Whereas Generation X was notorious for its complete distaste of marketing and branding, Millennials adore marketing, and tweens in particular can't get enough of it. However, it is equally important to note that tweens are smart. You will not put one over on them in the realm of advertising and promotion. They want to be a part of the creative process and want to know that you hear them; however, don't try to pull a fast one on them.

Visa Buxx Falls Flat with Tweens

Visa launched its Visa Buxx initiative in 2001 as a prepaid card for teens. In one of the original commercials, a parent walks

(continued)

(*continued*)

into a (dirty) teen bedroom, says the child needs to learn about financial responsibility, and hands the child the card.

However, it became almost instantly clear to consumers and competitors alike that Visa Buxx was not going to be popular with teens or with tweens. Why, you ask? Well, first of all, tweens are savvy and smart. They understand the need to save money. Even tweens who get a $9 weekly allowance know that they should save $1 of it for a rainy day. In focus group after focus group, tweens share that they're aware of saving. Second, the minute parents told their tweens what to do in the Buxx ad, the tweens were no longer interested. Parents were not viewed as hip and cool in 2001 as they are now. I call this the "*Desperate Housewives* effect." Not only did the show revive the career of actress Teri Hatcher, it also ushered into our psyche the idea of a glamorous, hip mom. And that has continued with shows like *Gossip Girl*, where hip Manhattanite parents have issues of their own. These parents aren't dowdy—they're cool. While Visa Buxx launched its product with great intentions, its communication to the consumer fell flat. Ten years later, the market is flooded with prepaid products. This was, most definitely, a missed opportunity.

We've talked about how fickle tweens can be, but the age-old question, "Do brands really matter?" is still a good one. The answer is *yes*, they absolutely do. According to "In the KidZone" (a research report by Decision Analyst and Hypothesis Group), brands really do matter to 6- to 17-year-olds. Topping the list as most important were video games (70 percent), restaurants (55 percent), and shoes (55 percent).

In our tween focus groups at Buzz Marketing, girls frequently affirm that they don't automatically trust generic health and beauty care items. They want to use brands that their friends know and trust. Retailers like girls' clothing line Justice are getting into this space and are even offering coupons for products that the stores do not carry, such as tampons. That kind of incentive certainly signals a trustworthy relationship with their customers.

Tweens also care about issues. A recent Buzz Marketing Group tween survey asked tweens what issues or social concerns they had, and responses included cyberbullying, parents, terrorism, substance abuse, and self-image. *Wow*. Tweens are sounding more and more like teens and young adults these days. They're aware of these issues, and in addition to the stress of school, they're dealing with some pretty serious concerns.

When tweens need to de-stress, they hang out with their friends and head to the mall—or at least go somewhere to shop. You see, malls aren't as popular with tweens as they used to be; for example, the majority of Justice stores are not mall-based. Shopping centers are increasing in popularity with tween shoppers and their parents. Another reason for this is that discounted or inexpensive retailers like Kohl's, Target, Walmart, and TJ Maxx are located there.

Let's look specifically at Kohl's for a moment. This retailer carries celebrity lines by Avril Lavigne, Britney Spears, and Lauren Conrad—the same three celebrities who always rank high on popularity lists with tweens. Target (or "*Tarjay*," as it's often called) is the place to go for affordable fashion, beauty, and electronics. Even though tweens are spending money, they're definitely value-conscious, and these stores offer a lot of product for the dollar.

Now that we understand where tweens are in their lives, how do marketers reach them effectively? Every successful Millennial marketing campaign should comprise four main qualities: It should be interactive, viral, educational, and value-based.

Millennials lead interactive lives, and they don't want to see static advertising campaigns. To that end, the first key ingredient for successful marketing campaign is *interactivity*. What is it that you want your target audience to do? Is your goal to generate sales? Raise awareness? Both? One does not always lead to the other, so you must be clear about what you want to accomplish. Remember, too, that Millennials want a relationship with your brand; they don't want to feel like you are merely talking *at* them. All solid relationships begin with good interaction and two parties openly communicating with each other. The same is true in marketing. In my opinion, there is no better example of an interactive marketing campaign today than Pepsi Refresh. I keep citing this campaign because it hits home in so many important areas when it comes to marketing to Millennials. By allowing users to both create their own ideas for funding and also vote on ideas from other consumers, Pepsi has created a dialogue.

A good campaign is also *viral*. Now, I'm sure you immediately think of Twitter, YouTube, and every other online tool as soon you hear "viral." That's not what makes something viral, though. It may help propel your campaign, but it's not the key. Think about why you tell something to your friends. It's usually because you think they need to know about it, right? For example, if you're reading a book that you love, you want other people to read it. If you just purchased the most comfy pair of sweatpants ever, you want your friends to be able to enjoy them as well. The key here is that the message is simple. You may simply love the characters in the book or adore the way that the sweatpants feel on you. Yet, too frequently, marketers want to communicate an excessive amount of messages in their advertising campaigns, which causes them to lose customers. At the end of the day, keeping it simple really does matter.

To cite another example, I'm amazed by the viral nature of singer Justin Bieber's accelerated career. Bieber rose to fame because his mom shot videos of him singing and posted them on YouTube. There was no flashy ad campaign with his face splattered all over Times Square, no appearances on late night TV shows (yet), and no radio play. Yet more than 1 million people loved what they saw. Whenever people talk to me about Justin Bieber, they all say the same thing: "That kid can really sing." Whether it's a tween or an adult, they are pulled in by a simple message.

Quality marketing campaigns are always *educational* as well. It might be as simple as the Gap showing off all of the new pants options for the new season, or Honda allowing users to build their dream car. You always consider what consumers can learn from your campaign, because this will also aid you in making it viral. People love to spread information, even when it's not all that positive. In fact, we've seen a few instances in which people were eager to spread negative information. When Gap recently decided to update its logo without providing an explanation, consumers fought back viciously—attacking the brand online via its Facebook page, tweeting about it, and commenting on blogs. Gap responded with both an apology and a return to the original logo.

Education and empowerment go hand in hand. The more that consumers know about your product or service, the more compelled they feel to be your brand ambassadors. But remember, this is a relationship. It goes both ways. A company like the Gap, with so many loyal and faithful consumers, could not make a major decision like that without feeling the heat.

Finally, a great ad campaign adds *value* in some way for the consumers. I've talked about intrinsic and extrinsic value, and a great example of this type of promotion is Dove's campaign for Real Beauty. I remember the first time I opened my favorite women's magazine to see a normal woman looking back at me. I thought about how beautiful she was and how beautiful she made me feel—and I obviously wasn't alone. It's been reported that the campaign has increased profits by over 700 percent for Dove.

Try to answer the following question when you're determining your value proposition: "What will consumers gain from this brand experience?" It's not always going to be a lofty statement. It might be something as simple as, "They will know how to style their hair better on a rainy day." If you want to convince Millennials to be committed to you, you have to dedicate yourself and your brand to interacting, educating, and adding value to their lives in some way.

Now that you have the keys to creating a good campaign, where do you launch it? I hate (yes, *hate*) statements like, "Print is dead." Another phrase on my hit list: "*No one watches TV anymore.*" Let me give you some quick facts from our tween buzzSpotter panel. Of our 624 survey respondents, 84 percent watch TV daily, with the top three networks being Disney (36 percent), Nickelodeon (31 percent), and Cartoon Network (18 percent). Contrast that with the 56 percent of respondents who go online daily and 38 percent who go online a few times each week, and you will see that tweens do, in fact, love their TV. If your budget can afford it, you need to be on TV, too.

What is it with this argument that print is dead? According to the "Power of Print" campaign, over 300 million people spend money on magazines in the United States, and you might be surprised to learn that the majority of those readers are under the age of 35. Indeed,

53 percent of our tween panelists engage in leisure reading. Books, too, are important. The top three series with tweens are *Diary of a Wimpy Kid, Harry Potter,* and *Percy Jackson.* So, it's important to engage with tweens in print as well as online. Magazines like *Girls' Life, Sports Illustrated for Kids,* and *J-14* all have millions of tween readers.

Spotlight: *J-14*

J-14 is a monthly magazine for girls ages 8 to 14 that is focused on entertainment, fashion, and beauty. Launched in 2000, it is published in the United States by Bauer Publishing, a division of the German company Bauer Verlagsgruppe. While monthly circulation is over 200,000, tween readers are in the *millions,* as the magazine enjoys a very healthy pass-along rate. It is successful because of its heavy focus on celebrities. *J-14* features dozens of celebrities each month that appeal to tweens' aspirational nature. Issues also include several pullout posters, offering a lot of value for the price. Even better, the magazine is a purchase that tweens can make with their own allowance, as it costs less than $5.

One medium for tween engagement that some might find shocking is the radio. Yes, even though 40 percent of our tween panelists own iPods and another 23 percent own MP3 Players, they are still listening to the radio on the journey to and from school and while on their computers. Tween-oriented stations on satellite radio and Radio Disney are popular ways to reach them as well. The key is to integrate radio ads into a bigger, more interactive campaign.

I'm aware that the big, sleeping giant in the room is the Internet. We know tweens are online—but which sites are they visiting? They love Disney.com, Nick.com, YouTube, Facebook, Webkinz.com, and Clubpenguin.com. These sites recognize the importance of user engagement. Tweens want to interact with your brands and to have an incentive to buy.

Here is one final caveat. Tweens, and Millennials in general, are just like the rest of us in that they love feeling a part of something exclusive.

The idea that they might miss out on something compels them to buy. One organization that understands this is the Girl Scouts of America. Every year, millions of boxes of Girl Scouts cookies are sold—not just because they're delicious, but because they are available for only a very limited season. You can even go to the Girl Scout web site and find a cookie rep on your street. Last year, more than 10 people were selling cookies in my development, so the Girl Scouts are ubiquitous yet exclusive at the same time. Now *that's* powerful marketing.

Even after you've done all of these things, you still have to contend with moms. A lot of brands operate under the notion that if a tween wants it, that's all that matters. While there may have been a time when this was true, parents are taking back the wallet power as we rise out of this recession; I can't emphasize enough how important it is to include attention to parents, particularly mothers, in advertising and promotion. Moms are very savvy; they truly know a whole lot about their children and what they want. Many companies and individuals have this image of moms who are disconnected from what their tweens want; however, nothing could be further from the truth. And moms also have viral power. Web sites like Momlogic.com and Mochamoms.org are major resources for moms, and they are great partners for marketers to expand their message.

BUZZFLASH: THE ART OF THE TRADE-UP, KID-STYLE

The folks at Nintendo are giving thousands of kids their first taste of a barter economy (albeit with some cash involved). During the spring of 2010, thousands of youngsters traded in their old Nintendo DSlite and DSi platforms for the next generation DSXL. The new model features bigger screens and more gaming capabilities, but has all the same favorite features that have made DS the best-selling handheld gaming device among kids. Turning in an old DS for a new one is not a brand-new concept at Nintendo (the company takes back the old device and issues a credit to be used against the purchase of

(continued)

(*continued*)

a new DS). But it is many tweens' first taste of trading up a product to which they've been fiercely loyal for a faster, better model from the same brand. It's an action they'll inevitably take with cell phones—and, in years to come, with cars—though the brand loyalty may be replaced by cost value. The arrival of the Dslite (which is slimmer than the original DS and has wireless features) and the DSi (which takes photos) sent old DS owners into stores in search of these later models. The DSXL's debut has kicked off a new wave of such trade-ups, giving many kids a lesson at the cash register they're sure to remember.

Teen spending has definitely been negatively impacted by the recession. In a survey of our buzzSpotters, 34 percent are currently employed, compared to 44 percent in 2009. It's important to first look at the source of today's teens' cash when considering their spending habits, especially in this current, troubled economy. Not surprisingly, 40 percent of today's youth rely primarily on their parents' income as their leading monetary source. This percentage is largely consistent with young people of the past two generations (X and Y). However, most young people nowadays understand the importance of working for what they want. Instead of having to ask for money each time they're ready to make a purchase, they're getting part-time jobs that allow them to call their own shots. Even though 40 percent still depend on their parents, almost as many (38 percent) say that they're earning it the hard way, with part-time jobs as their primary source of income.

Just having a job isn't always enough, though. A recent Pew study found that 31 percent of Millennials felt that they were earning enough money to lead the kind of lives they want. By contrast, 52 percent of 46- to 54-year-olds were satisfied with their current income. Even though they may not be satisfied with what they're earning, Millennials are still spending money.

Teens who spend their own money are often more selective than we'd expect. The plethora of product choices has created a culture that is often more concerned with getting a great deal than simply purchasing an item without regard for cost. This is due, at least in part, to more available price comparisons online. No past generation has had access to the interactive shopping process that's currently available to today's youth. They have the time to do their research, access to more retailers (traditional, niche/boutique, and online), and the desire to get great bargains for the exclusives they seek. Shopping may have become a bigger part of their everyday lives than in generations past, but so has becoming good at it.

Young people are also feeling the pinch of the current economic environment as much as the rest of us. They're giving up items that they were normally accustomed to purchasing, like those on the list at the beginning of this chapter. They're also finding it harder to obtain employment. Of our survey respondents, 44 percent had a job a year ago compared to 34 percent this year—a drop that is no doubt due to the diminishing labor market. With parents counting pennies and more and more young people looking for work, we can expect bargain shopping to continue, with plenty of price comparisons before purchase.

What makes the need for smart shopping even greater is the fact that 35 percent of our respondents claim to have 10 percent or less disposable total income. We're seeing a generation of teens who have a lot of purchasing options and often very little purchasing power. This has created a culture of cost-savvy, brand-loyal youth who are cognizant of their lack of cash and still find a way to get their favorite products at affordable prices.

It's too convenient to assume that the current generation of young people is made up of reckless spenders who disregard price tags and impulsively purchase whatever they can get their hands on. Older generations go to retail centers and see more choices, brands, and varieties than ever before, and they're buzzing with youth who seem to know their way through the shopping aisles as if they have them memorized. While it's true that teens are huge consumers of clothing, beauty products, food, and technology devices (where they get most of their entertainment), their extensive knowledge of their favorite products actually reflects the mind-set of a much older, wiser shopper. Instead of just browsing through the racks and shelves and picking out whatever feels right that day, young people are doing research online—and shopping there—to exhibit the kind of brand loyalty usually typical of a decade-long consumer.

The digital era helps extend this brand loyalty by providing platforms for products via both web sites and mobile devices to engage with the consumer. Young people in droves are using the Internet for shopping; a whopping 84 percent of respondents in our survey claim to shop online regularly. They likely enjoy the interactivity of shopping web sites and the availability of items that may not be in stock at their local retailer. The ease of use provided by the Internet serves as both a blessing and a curse for those brands seeking to build their brand image with younger customers. In a trend that will continue for the foreseeable future, companies will have to work increasingly harder to engage with Millennials. There are simply too many product choices, too many options for purchasing them easily, and a growing generation of intelligent shoppers who are putting brands under the microscope and forcing them to engage with their customer rather than just advertise their products. The World Wide Web opens many doors for a tech-savvy generation that is used to making quick, though calculated, decisions; however, it also offers a level of transparency to the process of checking price and quality that retailers have never before experienced.

Now, 39 percent of youth say they shop only when they need something instead of in periodic cycles. These individuals' attitude toward price and quality consciousness is becoming more prevalent in the marketplace and will continue to trend that way. They will quickly disregard luxury items that were once must-haves. Brands that ignore this new approach toward the purchasing process are going to be ignored by the youth in return. For example, once unstoppable retailer of preppy-but-hip teen clothing Abercrombie & Fitch stumbled horrendously by refusing to discount its product during the recession. Conversely, upstart Aéropostale, which kept prices low and lowered them even further, saw an explosion of growth on its web site; the company posted record sales as its stock price went up. Why? Kids quit the mall when Mom and Dad did, and no one was in the mood—or the financial position—to pay $80 for a hooded sweatshirt. Abercrombie saw its market share shrink and its stock take a nosedive, while Aéropostale went in the opposite direction—up, up, and away.

> **Marketing Moment:** Millennials no longer have to choose between value and style. They expect both from the brands that they love.

The need for brands to engage directly—via Web, mobile, creative campaigns—with young consumers who have a newfound price consciousness is certainly on the rise. However, there is another element that marketers must begin to implement into their launches and campaigns: aligning themselves with a cause, be it humanitarian or environmental.

Today's youth are less sheltered than in previous generations. While that's not always a good thing, it does mean that they are more in touch with adult-world concerns (e.g., the recession and environment) at an earlier age. This awareness extends into concern for the environment, disasters like the Haitian earthquake, family money woes, social injustice, and more. Many companies and organizations have successfully channeled these concerns into action—for example, Gap's Product Red campaign or Nickelodeon's Big Green Help.

Marketers often refer to the alignment of brands with social matters as "cause marketing." But due to the deeper level of engagement required for brands to earn the trust of their consumers, I'd now describe this as "cause consciousness." More direct engagement requires a deeper understanding of what teens stand for and what type of causes they want to support.

Which brands are getting it right? Well, the following are just a few. Some have been mentioned at great length in this book thus far, and others appear for the first time in this list. I hope that as you develop your marketing plans, you look at what these brands are doing to appeal to Millennial consumers.

1. **MTV.** Yes, we all know that MTV is supercool. But even supercool brands can take a serious dive. As a pioneer that's celebrated for showcasing diversity, MTV is responsible for bringing us shows like *The Real World*, which in its inception in the 1990s introduced Millennials to serious issues like

racism, abortion, and homosexuality. MTV also innovated in live show formats and introduced us to VJs and, most recently, the first TJ (Twitter jockey).

But just two years ago, MTV was under fire yet again. Ratings were sinking, and a lot of people had simply had enough of the single-note tonality of the network. So MTV again did what it does best—it innovated. The network realized that its audience craves many different shows in a variety of formats, and it listened to what was going on in the lives of its viewers. Thus, it might make sense that a show like *Jersey Shore*, which can initially seem repulsive at best, resonates with a generation of Millennials, who are watching their own families split up and fail. To Millennials, the show is about a modern-day family that will do anything for each other, not caricature-like Italians, as they've often been called. It's also clear that the cast members love themselves—a lot. And what teenager isn't looking for positive self-esteem? MTV has also relaunched a heavy-duty public-service campaign titled "A Thin Line," one of the best and most carefully thought out efforts to educate and arm Millennials in their fight against cyberbullying. MTV is at its best right now, and marketers can afford to snag a few pages from their book.

2. **Coca-Cola.** Coca-Cola marketers love to say that Coke is "125 years young," and it's that mentality that consistently puts Coke ahead of its competitors. Consider the fact that Coca-Cola sells 1.5 billion servings *per day*, which is, astoundingly, the equivalent of every person on planet Earth consuming a Coke once per week. In a recent presentation at a TED conference (a small nonprofit focused on ideas worth sharing), Melinda Gates said that we can all learn something from Coca-Cola's marketing strategies, and she highlighted three areas in which the brand excels: real-time data, a plugged-in global network of entrepreneurial talent, and incredible marketing. There's a more in-depth case study on Coca-Cola in Chapter 8, about global mobiles, but suffice it to say, there is no more effective global marketer than this company.

3. *Teen Vogue.* You may be wondering how *Teen Vogue* landed on this list, and in such a high position. I, for one, believe that *Teen Vogue* almost put *Vogue* out of business, and it has caught up to *Seventeen* in just a few short years—despite the fact that *Seventeen* had an almost 100-year lead! How does this happen? Well, *Teen Vogue* is a pioneer in mind-set marketing. Of course, you might think, *after all, their target is teens.* But is it totally? I don't think so. This publication has established itself as a resource for girls, teens, and young women who aren't ready for *Vogue.* Whereas *Vogue* feels unapproachable, *Teen Vogue* feels like your hip younger sister who has the best fashion advice. Throw in a brilliant partnership with MTV's hit show *The Hills,* and it all starts to make sense. *Teen Vogue* consistently attracts more advertisers than any other book in the space. Even high-end brands like Marc Jacobs and Louis Vuitton are there. *Vogue,* very cleverly, is fighting back. Its cover girls this year include stars like Blake Lively, Anne Hathaway, and Carrie Mulligan, all of whom seem better suited for a *Teen Vogue* cover, if you ask me.

4. **Old Navy**. While Old Navy may not be the most fashionable brand with teens (that would be American Eagle Outfitters), it sure does sell a lot of merchandise to them. How is this possible? Well, it helps that the brand is ubiquitous. It's *absolutely everywhere.* Old Navy has not only perfected the art of the marketing mix, it has also figured out how to add value. Its ad campaigns are humorous and viral, and its "$5 special of the week" hits home for Millennials. Although Old Navy would love to claim to be a major fashion player, it's really not. Other brands are setting style trends; Old Navy is where you go to get them for a good price, and that's okay. That's actually better than okay, considering the balance sheet.

5. **Apple**. Here's an interesting fact about Apple computers: They consistently rank higher than PCs when it comes to the cool factor, despite the fact that almost 70 percent of our surveyed buzzSpotters own PCs. That shift has occurred over the past year and is solely due to the recession. Millennials just can't afford to buy expensive products from the brand they love so

much. It's not like Apple is hurting, but imagine if the company could capture the revenue lost from Millennials who just can't afford its products! The iPod is still the MP3-playing device of choice (poor Zune), and that's not going to change anytime soon. Record companies should have taken some of that energy they put into fighting with consumers over illegal file sharing and used it to fight with Apple over iTunes—because they now own the downloading market. There will always be competitors, but they will never overpower Apple. There is just something this company knows about how to talk to and reach consumers.

It's all about product design at Apple. The company engineers focus on making really cool stuff and let that cool stuff do the talking. Even though 62 percent of our teen respondents have no use for an iPad, they think they're cool. They may not be buying one today, but in a few years, they'll be powering up with a $2,000 MacBook Pro—or whatever new machine Apple offers by then.

6. **Nintendo.** Nintendo is indeed back on top as a gaming console. After years of Sony PlayStation domination and Microsoft's Xbox popularity, Nintendo once again reigns supreme with Millennials. In our recent buzzSpotter tween survey, over 70 percent of respondents owned a Wii, while an additional 21 percent owned a DS or DSi. That's a lot of Nintendo for one tween! Even though 62 percent of respondents watch TV more than they play video games, I believe that girls are gaming more. Nintendo DS comes in girl-friendly colors like pink, blue, and silver, and the company also offers girl-friendly games. Still, more girls preferred Nintendo Wii than boys, who preferred DS. Nintendo is embracing the gaming culture of girls, which will be important to any video game maker who wants to sustain sales in the future.

7. **Nike.** This is yet another brand propelled by younger tween Millennials. In the quarterly KidZone report (a joint venture between Decision Analyst and Hypothesis Group), Nike was highlighted as the number one shoe brand among three groups: children 6 to 8, tweens 9 to 12, and teens 13 to 17.

What's fascinating, though, is that Air Jordans still ranked fourth on this list, across the board, as its own separate category, when major brands like Puma didn't even crack the top five. Wow. Nike's iconic logo and simple message, "Just do it," has always resonated with this age group. The brand also forges partnerships with iconic athletes like Michael Jordan and LeBron James. Nike is ubiquitous, and its branding is incredible. It never rests. The company understands that Millennials are elusive, that you have to work hard for their dollar every single day. Nike seems to live by the phrase, "Innovate or die," and its passion for product is its key to success. Nike uses that knowledge to inform consumers' purchases.

8. **T-Mobile**. Even though T-Mobile trails competitors AT&T, Verizon, and Sprint, it's still the coolest. When is the last time you heard a Millennial go on and on about how cool AT&T is? Probably not recently. While Millennials might love the brand's phones, phones per se aren't really exclusive (with the brief exception of the iPhone, which will launch with Verizon in 2011). As a brand, T-Mobile resonates not just with its 34 million U.S. subscribers, but with Millennials in general. T-Mobile understands the power of TV and advertising. It launched a 2009 campaign with Charles Barkley, Dwayne Wade, and Dwight Howard. The company has also worked with Catherine Zeta-Jones, and it sponsors athletic events, musical festivals, and European football.

9. **Axe**. Though Old Spice may have launched a juggernaut of a campaign in 2010, Axe still reigns supreme with Millennials. Launched by Unilever as a deodorant brand in 1983, the line now includes shower gels, aftershaves, skin care, colognes, and shampoo. Axe ad campaigns are known among Millennials for being very tongue in cheek. Campaigns like "World's Manliest Rituals," in partnership with web site Funny or Die, further the brand's snarky approach. Remember that tidbit about Preppies and conformism? Axe completely understands that basic need. It very clearly says, "Hey guys, if you do *this*, you can expect *that* from girls." 'Nough said.

10. **Louis Vuitton**. I know what you're thinking. What Millennial can afford Louis Vuitton? Well, teens and young adults, for sure. But before we go into *why* they're buying, let's talk about the brand's appeal. For tweens, it's aspirational; for teens, it's inspirational. Seeing ad campaigns featuring their favorite celebrities and causes is totally inspiring. It's a reflection of how young adults see themselves. It's also a badge of self-fulfillment. It's hard to believe that a luxury brand can resonate so much with Millennials, even in a recession. Yet we're finding that teens are entering the luxury market with smaller, less expensive items, in the $200 range. That means they're shopping more at discount stores for the basics and adding some glamour to their looks with Louis Vuitton.

Louis Vuitton has done a lot to capture its Millennial audience. Whether it's through a faux graffiti collection or Kanye West rapping about the brand on one of his many hit records, the company has found a way to resonate with its younger audience. Really, though, it's just the genius of Marc Jacobs, who would have been next on this very list, for his brand Marc by Marc Jacobs. Marketers can learn a big lesson from Jacobs. Just because Millennials can't afford to buy a $30,000 Louis Vuitton trunk doesn't mean they won't plunk down $70 for a fragrance. If you get them while they're young, they'll be loyal for life.

TINA'S TOP FIVE

1. *Millennials still rely heavily on retail therapy—and they will keep shopping.* Just because we're in the midst of an economic downturn doesn't mean the purse holders to parents' discretionary income aren't still active in the marketplace. In fact, they're more active than ever; they're becoming smarter shoppers and using tools available (web sites, promotional offers, etc.) at increasing rates. We can expect this kind of active shopping experience to

continue as brands do more with interactive platforms to make the process easier and the choices more obvious.

2. *Although they're still spending, they're pickier than ever.* The increase in digital shopping options adds layers to teens' decision-making process. One layer also related to the digital experience is the fact that young people can now easily share information about an item on sale or something they don't like about a product. This creates a quagmire for retailers, who must engage aggressively yet pay even more attention to quality and customer satisfaction. Digitally, news of a negative shopping experience often travels faster than news of a satisfied customer.

3. *If you want to sell to Millennials, be prepared to work really, really hard for the sale.* Brands can't get away with simply advertising and pushing their products anymore. They have to make contact with potential customers, get to know them, and then quickly show them how their brand fits with shoppers' needs. The world of mega-advertising is being swallowed by widespread yet cautious selling. While young people have to work harder to find jobs and must cope with the reality of less pocket money, brands are going to have to work hard to reach out to young people, get involved in their lives, and relate to their problems.

4. *Millennials are more value- and cost-conscious now than they have ever been.* Being cost-conscious is nothing new, especially when times are tight. But getting value for products and services is taking on a new meaning. The contemporary definition of value includes direct customer engagement through a variety of digital tools, accessibility through a vibrant online marketplace, and an understanding of your target audience's underlying social views. Just as teens are constantly developing their tastes for fashion and entertainment, brands will now also have to regularly reinvent themselves and their approach to marketing.

5. *Millennials no longer have to choose between value and style. Many new companies entering the market provide style at a great price*

(continued)

(continued)

(e.g., Uniqlo, Forever 21, H&M). The most shopping-savvy generation in history is not foolish. They price-shop heavily, and they know what it takes to produce a lot of the products they buy. For example, teens' understanding of technology and software at an early age helps them gauge which new gadgets are overpriced and still in their early stages of functionality. Young girls with their own fashion blogs and clothing lines are starting to learn how much it costs to create a new sun dress line in the summer, and they aren't going to pay you much more for it when they know how to make it themselves.

Responses received by tween panelists from 2010 buzzOn Tweens Study.

4

"I Texted You :)"

Screen Time, All the Time: How Technology Is Rewiring the New Millennial

BUZZSPOTTER PROFILE

Jenna was incredibly excited to finally be on Facebook. It took forever to assure her parents that the site was safe and that all her friends were on it. Supercool profile pic? Check. More than 500 friends? Check. Ultrahumorous anecdote for what's on your mind? Double check.

Jenna hops on her bike and rides it the half mile to her superposh high school. She kisses her swim captain boyfriend on the cheek and they head into homeroom hand in hand. She tosses her boho-chic Target hobo across the back of her chair and opens up her iPhone.

Jenna's face turns ghostly white when she sees her supposed friend Gail's status update: Interested in joining the Ho's for Homecoming group? Call Jenna at—and there's her cell phone number, listed for every single one of Gail's 563 friends to see.

Not exactly the Facebook welcome Jenna was hoping for.

 Pop Quiz

True or False: The majority of teens want an iPad.

More than 1 billion text messages are sent every day, many of them by tweens and teens. Nearly half of all 8- to 18-year-olds text daily, sending on average 118 messages and spending about 90 minutes on texting and receiving.[1] That is a lot of data! If technology is a language, today's Millennials speak it fluently, while the rest of us are just playing catch up. Technology, and Millennials' preoccupation with it, gets a bad rap. I believe it's mostly because we don't truly understand it. We may use it, but it was a disruptive innovation in our lives; it hasn't always been with us. I've spent the last few chapters talking about how to attract Millennials, what they want from brands, and brands that are getting it right. But to truly understand Millennials and get it right, you have to understand their relationship with technology.

If most kids are hearing about new products online, and if they prefer watching content online to watching it on TV and prefer blogs to magazines, then how do we reach them? In a recent Buzz Marketing Group survey, we wanted to understand the effects of technology on this demographic. The information is staggering. Of our teen buzzSpotter respondents, 54 percent prefer blogs to magazines (remember, this doesn't mean magazines aren't important, because 46 percent still prefer them). This is a bigger trend with teen male respondents (63 percent) than teen female (55 percent of whom prefer magazines to blogs). The big jump is in TV versus Internet. A whopping 84 percent prefer the Internet to TV. Of course, you might say, well, they had to choose between the two. That's true, but in their everyday lives, they're making these choices. They might be watching their favorite TV shows online, or even via their DVR, but it's no secret that live TV viewership is down overall, and down especially with Millennials. They want their content when and how it's convenient for them.

Later in this chapter we're going to take a look at the Facebook effect—what happens when kids put too much information about their personal lives out there in cyberspace and come to regret it. There was a time when *text* was a noun, and terms like *cyberbullying* and *sexting* weren't in any dictionary (even Urbandictionary.com). All that exposure often comes with a hefty price tag, whether kids are perfectly innocent or their Facebook page is a screaming reminder of questionable extracurricular activities.

The relevant buzzword here is *Warholism*: the belief many new Millennials hold that fame (or notoriety) is a possibility for them at some point in their lives, whether it's via Facebook, YouTube or, for the truly motivated, at the movie-star level. For example, megastar and teen pop music sensation Justin Bieber got his start after his mother posted numerous homemade videos on YouTube. There seem to be more "real" people on TV these days than walking down the street. There was a time in the early 1990s when your only shot at being on TV was as a game-show contestant or as one of the lucky seven cast members on MTV's *Real World*. How times have changed. If marketers don't understand what Wharholism and the Facebook effect are doing to this consumer, they might miss the mark on their advertising.

There was a time when everyone wanted to look like Tyra Banks or Christy Turlington. Models are still relevant, and probably always will be, but they don't have the same effect on the younger generation. Older Millennials don't want to be *like* them, they want to *be* them. We'll discuss this more later, when I spotlight Kim Kardashian.

No discussion on Millennials and technology would be complete without exploring the myth of the wired, unengaged kid. You know, the one who supposedly sits in his or her room and plays video games, goes on Facebook, or Skypes for 12 hours at a time, earbuds firmly in place 24/7. Yes, some kids do fit this profile; however, the numbers show that most young people are learning to make the technology adapt to their needs—not the other way around. We also explore this trend.

Is technology the face of the Millennial generation? With Facebook, faces on video chats, faces on chat icons and profile pictures, face recognition, and so forth, it's hard to argue otherwise. The Millennials— by far the most tech-savvy bunch on the planet—appear to be in a face-off with technology's many offerings, for better or worse.

Respondents were asked in a recent Pew Research Center study on Millennials ages 18 to 29, "What makes your generation unique?" Researchers also posed this question to Gen Xers, baby boomers, and the Silent Generation. The top response (14 percent) among Silents was "World War II and the Depression;" for boomers (17 percent) it was "work ethic." Gen Xers are the first to say "technology use" made their generation unique; 12 percent gave this answer. But twice as many Millennials ranked "technology use" as the factor that gave them a distinct identity from previous generations. If Pew were to poll the youngest Millennials right now, I'd bet that "technology use" would play an even larger role in how they define themselves. I'm quite sure about that, because I just finished asking this very group about their use of technology in our annual teen study, and here are the results:

- 98 percent of our respondents have a cell phone; more than half use it for texting, while only 9 percent use it for phone calls.
- 40 percent spend three to six hours online; 39 percent spend one to three hours online.

- 72 percent get their news online.
- 61 percent hear about new products online, while 15 percent still hear about them from friends.
- 80 percent own laptops, and nearly 90 percent own iPods and digital cameras.

Whereas most of us still remember when computer screens were still a new addition to the home and the workplace, today's kids watch *iCarly* on their parents' iPhones or the *Hotel for Dogs* DVD on a built-in screen in the family minivan, while their older counterparts capture images and send text messages on their cell phones. Indeed, wireless industry association CTIA estimates that texting is up by 50 percent in the past year alone. According to one survey, text-sending teens are the fastest-growing segment of the wireless industry.[2]

In many respects, the Millennials have no choice but to designate technology as their generation's theme. The world has repeatedly witnessed technological innovations over the past 20 years that were, until recently, completely unimaginable. Both the quality and quantity of technical devices and applications have grown at an exponential rate, and today's youth are born into a culture that promises speed (think *instanity*) and devices designed to be personalized.

Innovations in connecting the world in real time that can be tailored to users' desires have spawned various new ways of interacting. Although we have a variety of mobile discussion methods at our disposal (voice calls, instant chat, and e-mail), texting, in particular, poses the biggest challenge to traditional communication. The world has always relied on the quality of a written exchange over a verbal one, for both communication and recording purposes. Until fairly recently, cell phones were a rarity, and most people were still contacting one another via longer written messages. Now, the boom of texting, or SMS, is giving rise to shorter, yet more frequent, text bytes that are replacing longer verbal conversations. A recent Pew study found that 59 percent of all Americans send or receive text messages. Worldwide, 2.4 billion people send or receive text messages—74 percent of all cell phone users! But here is one interesting fact: In our recent buzzSpotter survey, we found that only

9 percent say the primary use of their phone is voice chats, which contrasts with the fact that in a recent Pew study, only 9 percent of the Silent Generation send text messages.[3] How's that for polar opposites! It's amazing what can happen in a few generations. We can only imagine what the children of Millennials will be doing.

Letters are being removed from words or, along with numbers, are replacing them entirely. Consider, "I hav smthng 4 u when I c 2 u ltr." Having trouble translating? Well, you'd better start learning, and fast. You may also start seeing "omg" (Oh my God) and "cc" (carbon copy) in e-mails or other messages or in reference to the latest popular music. Make no mistake: These personalized, shortened forms of exchange are rapidly entering the mainstream. Twitter made texting public by allowing users to notify followers of their location and activities with short, often cryptic, messages. These messages, or tweets, are also often made public on the user's Twitter profile page.

Twitter's ability to reach larger audiences—and therefore to influence culture more quickly—emphasizes a highly consistent theme among young people's technology use: mobility. Much like other popular Web-based applications such as Facebook, Twitter has flourished in popularity due to its buzzworthy usage and the fact that you can access it from anywhere, on any phone, device, or computer with wireless capability, at any time.

But don't assume that teens are tweeting away. Only 55 percent of our buzzSpotters are on Twitter. That probably sounds like a great number, but consider that 99 percent have a Facebook page.[4] Twitter, like the iPad, makes sense for certain types of people. It's more likely that professionals and young adults are using the iPad than their younger tween and teen counterparts. Consider that teens are used to sending messages to multiple people via their cell phones or their status updates on Facebook. Twitter's really not groundbreaking for them. But just because they're personally not users doesn't mean that they won't follow brands they love, especially when those brands are using Twitter to announce holiday sales and promotions. Twitter is a great way to communicate that type of information. It also costs you nothing. And if you're a new or emerging brand, you can now purchase promotional tweets to build an audience.

The mobile device has taken precedence over everything else in the hands of today's youth. Sure, laptops, home computers, and TVs still get plenty of burn time; however, teens leave them behind on their way to school, and they shut them off while playing games on their phones before bed. In addition to portability, mobile devices provide a crossroad for relationship management (via phone, text, and chat) and entertainment (Web, gaming, music). This combination provides a crucial opportunity for a teen to discover something new that he or she loves—a new game, song, or even just a piece of information found online—and then *immediately* share it with friends. Welcome to word-of-mouth marketing on steroids. E-mails have replaced letters and phone calls, and texts (well, just letters and numbers, really) have replaced entire conversations.

Some people are skeptical about the impact that these new communication methods are having. Many are worried that they're negatively impacting our culture, diluting us to beings who rarely interact with any substance. However, I'd argue that we're witnessing a generation of individuals who are harnessing the world's information with their hands and collaborating about its problems, and potential solutions, with their fingertips. Over time, I believe that this growth in technical innovation—and therefore the speed and breadth of communication that it stimulates—will lead to an enhanced ability to take a deeper look at the problems we're facing, because we're all able to look at them together. It's also important to note that nearly all of these exchanges (messages, file sharing, and data transmission) are searchable, sortable, and storable. This excites me as a researcher and marketer when I think about the possibilities of finding new ways to use the raw data being produced by the world's youth, around the clock, to anticipate the upcoming trends in our culture. This generation is going to lead us into a new millennium filled with both possibility and fear—and we're going to get to read along with them in real time. Remember, one of Coca-Cola's keys to success is its ability to harness and utilize real-time data. That data doesn't always have to come in a sophisticated package; it can be as simple as paying attention to a Twitter feed for an hour.

If you explore a public timeline on Facebook or Twitter, you'll start to notice how much people are sharing with each other. While many users still provide pointless details about their day ("Heading to the gym now . . ."), there is also plenty of quality content being discussed and referenced ("Check out this cool YouTube video . . .) via links to the World Wide Web. The connectivity of these two worlds—social/ relationship management and entertainment—has spawned a marketing phenomenon, and only the Millennials truly understand how to use it to its fullest potential. But brands are picking up on it. Who is getting it right? Well, here are examples of three brands that are doing a great job of interacting with Millennials online:

1. **Victoria's Secret Pink.** With more than 7.7 million fans, Victoria's Secret Pink is one of the biggest brands on Facebook. The page is definitely specific to the products, and it showcases bras and panties, but there's also a fantastic social element to it. Fans can "send a sassy PINK element" to their friends via cards with phrases like "Kiss, Kiss, Wink, Wink" and "All Fun No Sleep." Very cheeky. They post photos from events and post invites to private shopping events. Fans feel like they're in an exclusive circle of friends. Definitely an amazing brand experience.

2. **Starbucks.** We all know how popular coffee is, so it shouldn't be surprising that Starbucks has more than 19 million fans on Facebook. Fans post all day long about their drink purchases, even posting pics of themselves (and their children) enjoying Starbucks beverages. The Fan Page really feels like it's driven by the consumers and their love for the coffee, not by a corporation trying to make a statement.

3. **Adidas.** The shoe company has more than 4.5 million Facebook fans between its Adidas and Adidas Football pages. Not too shabby. What's interesting about Adidas is that it does a great job of showcasing products and commercials while also allowing consumers to interact with its page. Adidas understands that the key to a great fan experience on Facebook is not to be too overbearing.

What can *your* brand do to interact better with Millennials on Facebook? First, don't be too corporate. Your Facebook page is not your company web site. You've come to *their* turf. Treat your page like it's an extension of a teen's friend network, not an advertising network. Second, offer something exclusive to your fans. It can be a discount code, exclusive video launch, *anything* that makes them feel like they're in the know. Finally, be engaging. Remember, this is a relationship that requires two-way communication. Ask your fans what they'll be doing for fun this weekend, or what new product designs they'd like to see. They will respond.

In addition to leisure screen time, like social networking and checking out YouTube, more and more Millennials perform academic-related tasks on a computer. It could simply be typing up a paper that they've researched online, or logging on to a teacher's homework page via a site like Blackboard.com, which connects students with their teachers and assignments. Once upon a time, the only high-tech device on a kid's school supply list was a calculator. Now kids need laptops to make the grade. And we're not just talking high school kids. This holiday season, Fisher-Price is releasing an $80 iPad-like device called the iXL that's a touch-screen computer for the juice-box generation.

Technology has invaded the scholastic market and is now so commonplace with young people that it is naturally reshaping the way all of us teach each other. The education industry largely determines how young people use technology as adults. If these teens and tweens start to use technology to manage their lives and make them easier—via calendars and scheduling, managing relationships, storing and organizing documents and files, conducting banking, and making payments online—then they'll naturally carry these habits forward with them when they become adults, which will in turn create a workforce of sharp, fast, and orderly people.

In May 2010, the National Center for Education Statistics released a report on the use of educational technology in schools. The results are astounding. It seems 97 percent of our school students have computers in the classroom, 93 percent of which have the Internet. Each computer serves an average of 5.3 students. There are also more primary school students with computers in their classrooms (98 percent) than secondary students (95 percent).[5]

It may not be surprising that computers are in our classrooms, but what about handheld devices? Digital cameras? Even iPods? Yes, those devices are there. In fact, 64 percent of teachers say digital cameras are available in their classrooms, as needed, and 49 percent use them sometimes or often. Furthermore, 18 percent say that iPods are available, as needed, and 36 percent use them sometimes or often. Even handheld devices, though sparse (8 percent have access to them), are used 50 percent of the time when they are available. So, teachers are doing what it takes to keep up with the technological level of their students.

While teachers are catering to the technological needs of their students, they still have to deal with those short attention spans. This is a major issue for Millennials, and, unfortunately, they carry it into the career world after college. When younger people enter the working world, which is much less structured than school, they may be bored and unmotivated by the lack of multiple things to do at once. I wonder how present-day Millennials' bosses will respond when new employees demand to listen to music on their earbuds while typing out an important memo for a client. In fact, they might even claim that it *helps* them focus on the memo. Is this illogical, or just a culture shift? It would probably be wise for bosses in such situations to listen to their employees. After all, they know themselves better than anyone else does. Give the Millennials' method a try, and see how they perform before rejecting new working habits or environments just because they are foreign to you and not the way you're accustomed to working.

This is going to be especially important for younger Millennials, who spend more time looking at screens than doing much else. Indeed, a recent Buzz Marketing Group report found that 98 percent of tweens were online a few times each week, and 56 percent were every day.[6] In our Buzz Marketing Group focus groups, feedback from tweens about their online habits makes it clear that they're doing many, many things at once. They love to play video games, chat with friends, listen to music, Google things, and shop. And they're doing it all simultaneously.

Despite a few generational differences along the company ladder, we have seen that companies offering technology incentives—such as providing discounts or promotions to use certain devices (iPhones, BlackBerrys), upgrading and updating computer systems, or allowing some freedom in their employees' online usage while working—are having an easier time in both recruiting and keeping younger employees. This type of company culture, of course, also trickles down to the consumers, who recognize that certain companies are "cool" not only because they create products, but also because of how they treat their employees. Online shoe and clothing retailer Zappos.com has probably enjoyed as much press concerning its company culture and office environment as it has for the breadth of its product catalog (oh, and it's also famous for its excellent customer service).

Brands are acknowledging the mobile craze's presence by creating "byte-size" versions of their products and advertisements that can be displayed on smaller screens and accessed through mobile Web portals. We're currently experiencing a boom in the use of applications—that is, add-ons to current computer programs and platforms that are more lovingly referred to as *apps*. Along with the BlackBerry, Apple's devices in particular have encouraged users to download these functions. Apple's software developers have squeezed tiny program applications into pieces of downloadable data, which are available through App Stores and are accessible for a few dollars or less each. This trend is expected to persist, as the functional use of computing devices continues to penetrate niche functionality while offering users the chance to play cards on their phones, remix a music track on their iPads, and so on.

Spotlight: XIPWIRE—Introducing the Mobile Wallet

In keeping up with the revolutionized world of technology and its users, XIPWIRE has created an easy-to-implement and cost-effective service that allows people to send and receive money via text messaging. "Convenience is the new black, which is driving mobile money to its tipping point," says Sibyl Lindsay,

XIPWIRE cofounder. "[Millennials] are not going to take the time to sit down and write a check because they are too busy managing their life on their cell phones. They're using their phones for everything else, so why should they put it down to pay?" Great point. Another great service for nonprofits? XIP2GIVE, which allows nonprofits to receive guaranteed text donations. For the first time, thanks to text donations, charities and nonprofit organizations are looking at Millennials as viable donors. The Obama campaign showed us the power of microgiving, and a service like XIPWIRE is next natural platform.

At the beginning of this chapter, we asked our pop quiz question about teens' desire to have an iPad. Were you surprised that most teens do *not* want an iPad? After all, most of us assume that young people desire the "newest thing," regardless of what the device actually *does*. However, the fact is that, although teens indeed crave updated and advanced gadgets, their desire stems from the actual innovations and upgrades—not just the date on the box. Young people today tend to buy technology that meets particular needs or suits major interests. A student who loves music and fashion may have a device that allows for audio recording and sampling, along with quick-launch buttons, maybe even apps, for their favorite retailers' e-commerce web site and RSS feeds (i.e., data updates from across the Web) of new music releases and clothing launches.

Why aren't today's teens going for the iPad in droves? After all, it's a great device built for viewing and browsing *anything* online. However, despite the fact that the device is phenomenal for these these core activities, which are its focus, the iPad lacks some other key features that are extremely important to on-the-go teens—including a camera to Skype, chat, and take pictures and the ability for quick social networking tweets and status updates (because a mobile with a keyboard for thumbing is probably going to allow teens to tweet, update, and text more quickly). For these reasons, on the average

Millennial's list of tech must-haves, the iPad still falls below smaller mobile devices (including the iPhone, the iPad's "junior"). Until the next version (and depending on feature upgrades), the first iPad will likely be used mostly by those who tend to peruse Web pages longer than teens do: professionals.

This brings to mind another trend: the "hand-me-up." Yes, as teens and tweens become bored with their cell phones, they're handing them *up* to Mom and Dad! With family plans so prevalent, it's easy for this shuffle to happen. The trend makes sense. Devices like the iPad make sense for their parents, who really have no interest in reading the *New York Times* on a screen smaller than a postcard. An iPad makes complete sense to them. Who knows, maybe parents will be the ones handing down their iPads to their teen and tween children!

When discussing technology with older groups, I often hear the lament, "Young people are faster at this stuff than I am." These advanced generations are still struggling with the fact that they've spent most of their lives doing one or two things at a time. Computers and user-friendly interfaces (e.g., minikeyboards and touch screens) have opened up the possibility to tackle multiple tasks at once. Yes, today's youth are spending a lot of their screen time multitasking. What looks like chaos to us—simultaneously doing homework, Skyping, and texting, all while listening to music—is simply the norm for them. It's just another facet of *instanity*.

Marketing Moment: Screenagers

We must understand that today's Millennials are "screenagers,"* always consumed by and actively engaged with a screen of some type, be it a mobile phone, computer, or television. Brands have to recognize the opportunity in this abundance of screen time through technical devices and not ignore the need for a full integration of technology when considering a marketing strategy. Whether you're selling soap or Silly Bandz, full integration of technology is imperative. Tech cannot be an add-on; it must be the nucleus from which you work any marketing campaign. Millennials won't have it any other way.

---

*Term coined by Media theorist Douglas Rushkoff in his 2006 book, *Screenagers: Lessons In Chaos From Digital Kids.*

The Facebook Effect (and an Introduction to Warholism)

In the beginning of this chapter, I mentioned the *Facebook effect*— that is, what ensues when kids put too much of their personal lives in the public domain on the World Wide Web and come to regret it later.

For starters, the Facebook effect has extremely serious societal consequences that may supersede some of the previously cited constructive uses for technology in school and at work. The need for stardom and attention has made young people more self-conscious and narcissistic. Their public image on Facebook becomes more important than who they truly are as people. Many focus more intently on building a "brand" of themselves than they do on building life skills, practicing music or sports, and reading and doing their homework. Of course, as they get older, the pictures may begin to portray parties, involvement with illegal substances, and interaction with people with whom they may one day regret associating.

It's not that previous generations didn't participate in bad behavior. Quite the contrary! (Hippies, anyone?) They just didn't document every single happening, all day long. There comes a point when too much sharing is really just too much. I believe that later in life, Millennials will come to regret sharing so much of their lives in the public realm and will seek their privacy by any means necessary. All things are cyclical, and right now, we're in a cycle of oversharing, but we need to be prepared for what will happen when Millennials decide to seek their privacy.

For now, we live in a world where people wait with bated breath for the next tweet from Kim Kardashian, Nicole Richie, and Ashton Kutcher. Interestingly enough, Kutcher made history as the first celebrity to e-mail over 1 million tweeps, or Twitter followers.

Spotlight: Kim Kardashian

If you peruse her wiki (her online listing on Wikipedia), you'll find that Kim Kardashian is "an American celebutante, social-ite, television personality, producer, actress, and model." Her wiki goes on to say that she's the daughter of attorney Robert Kardashian and that she is also known for her sex tape with singer Ray J. Let's stop there. To many, their first introduction to Kim Kardashian is through her sex tape. There was a time in our culture when such a thing was career ending. In this case, can you argue that it was career *making*? You could. Before her own sex tape, she was just a member of Paris Hilton's sex tape. Afterward? Paris *who*? One thing you can't dispute is that Kim Kardashian is a marketing maven. She took a massive pile of lem-ons and made multimillion-dollar lemonade. She will have the last laugh, but you have to wonder how many Millennials look at her story and see sex tapes and sexting as just means to a finan-cial end. Kardashian consistently calls her tape "embarrassing" and a "personal low," but she's apparently flying high now.

Discussing the modern possibilities of instant fame via the Web and social networking online allows me to introduce a concept that I call *Warholism*—a cultural tendency among young people (and a few older ones) characterized by an obsession with fame and a desire to attract attention in any way possible. Everything these individuals do must be a spectacle—preferably one that's recorded for YouTube. Social norms on behaviors considered "outrageous" and "taboo" are bend-ing as younger people expose more of their private lives and show a willingness to perform mindless and sometimes daring antics.

There are, of course, many potential downsides to this kind of social omnipresence. Advertising one's personal habits and style preferences on a digital basis puts young people in danger of opening the door to predators who might attempt to contact and manipulate them. Stories of *sexting* (sending sexually explicit messages or photographs between mobile phones) and *cyberbullying* (using technological information and communication to bully) are starting to make headlines in far too many of our nation's newspapers. I've been speaking and blogging about these subjects for years. The Facebook effect allows predatory individuals, whether they have criminal/sexual aspirations or simply want to harass innocent people, an opportunity to gather valuable information about their prey and use it against them. This depraved practice is unfortunately becoming increasingly common, because it often builds upon itself. Once someone is digitally persecuted or harassed, especially at a young age, he or she may switch from victim to aggressor; it is so easy to do something to someone else once it's been done to us. All these young people have to do is go online, look over the information of someone they know, and start to pick on that person.

I'm a staunch advocate of putting into place policies against cyberbullying and sexting at all levels, from the federal government to local communities. The people who propagate this kind of vindictive harassment are growing in number, and they need to be educated on how harmfully these actions impact others. In some cases, they are single-handedly drawing attention away from the great uses of technology for the Millennials and instead emphasizing how destructive certain devices and web sites can be.

I have to give credit to MTV, which launched "A Thin Line," a campaign against digital abuse. MTV's campaign "is a multi-year effort empowering America's youth to identify, respond to, and stop the spread of digital abuse."[7] What I appreciate most is that MTV took the time to actually conduct research with Millennials to find out the extent of digital abuse among them. The statistics are staggering. The study, conducted jointly by MTV and the Associated Press, found that 50 percent of 14- to 24-year-olds have been the target of some form of digital abuse. Even more alarming is that 3 in 10 have sent or received nude pictures of their peers online or via cell phone. And 61 percent of those who admitted to sexting felt pressured to do so.[7]

What did MTV do with this information? It built a coalition of leading authorities, such as Parry Aftab and Esta Soler, to discuss the topics of sexting, digital dating abuse, and cyberbullying. It is also engaging its audience through thought-provoking public service announcements, integration into top MTV shows, innovative online and mobile tools, curricula, and more. MTV is also engaging celebrities. Stars who have already joined the cause as ambassadors include Rosario Dawson, Asher Roth, Jessica Stroup, and Michelle Trachtenberg. The campaign also offers thought-provoking slogans. My favorite: "It's a thin line between delete/forward." Wow. That's a powerful message.

It appears that Millennials are responding to the campaign. More than 8.3 million viewers watched the special *Sexting in America: When Privates Go Public* when it premiered on February 14, 2010. The special has reached a total of more than 18 million viewers. As a result of the campaign, more than 600,000 Millennials have already taken some form of action to stop digital abuse.

Even though digital abuse is happening, let's not assume that all effects of technology are negative. There are also some positive aspects to the Facebook effect. People have posed counterarguments that the increased exposure to more information allows younger people to learn more, and more quickly, about themselves and the world in which they live. However, in either case, it appears that young people are increasingly growing into one of the four main tribes during early adolescence, then branching off into their own tribal offshoots. They can enjoy whatever information and entertainment they want, but when it comes time to choose up sides at school, most of them follow along with the tribes already in place. They're essentially waiting to blaze their own trails until later, after they've had a chance to develop their opinions further. This is somewhat disappointing and even scary, in my opinion; after all, the most successful people are usually willing to take risks (and be themselves). I started a company at 16 because I was ambitious and found a hot idea, not because I was following the lead of my peers.

Arguably the biggest upside to the Facebook effect is that younger people are able to learn more about each other and their world at a pace never experienced before. Of course, teens and tweens will always learn from each other and be influenced by their peers' opinions. However, we must carefully consider an important fact: that the openness of the information age is providing *too many* opinions at once, thereby minimizing the time that a young person has for self-reflection and personal development. It seems that the human mind can justify almost anything and entertain any notion. The information floodgates are wide open, and there aren't many guides out there instructing young people on how to navigate the waters. That's why it's absolutely vital for parents and youth leaders to take the initiative here—not only to monitor these Millennials' online usage and communications, but also to educate them on the consequences of overexposing personal information online. One point that has yet to hit home among all generations is this: All of the information that we put online is being archived somewhere. It will likely not be erased in our lifetimes. *All of it*—every last photo, tweet, update, and post is out there somewhere. Be careful about what you say and what you display.

Brands and companies also need to pay attention to the cluttered information marketplace and make sure their messages stick out in meaningful, and not annoying, ways. Companies like Mozes, which allows brands to connect with their customers via cell, are great partners for digital engagement. Like it or not, we trust these brands—as participants in the digital marketplace—to help determine what younger generations are talking about and how they are spending their time. Oftentimes, their messages are more powerful than those of friends and family.

Spotlight: Mozes

Launched in April 2006, Mozes was originally created to gain more information about a search subject through a mobile phone. Since that initial launch, Mozes has morphed into the largest

(*continued*)

(*continued*)

mobile phone connection between artists, brands, and fans that exists today. Its mission is to "connect our customers to billions of people at the points of inspiration." The company focuses on connecting brands and consumers on mobile devices in the areas of entertainment and live events. Mozes has partnered with the likes of Rascal Flatts, Justin Bieber, Portland Trailblazers, Rock the Vote, Virgin Mobile, and Ford.

Always Online: The Unengaged Tech Addict

Almost all of us know someone like this. These tech addicts are usually quiet, introverted, and may not look like they get outside very much. As a result, they have more trouble making friends, participating around the house, and taking part in popular after-school activities. They seemingly don't know how to communicate with their peers and appear to frequently "think in code." As a result, they tend to keep to themselves and lack basic social skills. Because these kids don't always get a healthy amount of human interaction, they're usually picked on so much that they recede even further into the dark tech world in which they live, constantly interacting online or gaming. Yet ironically, this is the group who receives the most attention when problems need to be solved, when a new device needs unlocking or troubleshooting, or when a teacher needs a standout student to explain something that the rest of the class simply cannot do. They may be on computers more, but they likely are doing more of their homework as well (and doing it quickly). In other words, they are consumed by their gadgets because the technology they are using is much more complex and stimulating than their schoolwork. They're bored with school and consider it to be a side project (albeit one that many of them still manage quite well). If this group makes it through high school with a decent group of friends (yes, even fellow nerds count), they'll likely go on to better colleges than their peers and set themselves up for the future because they have been practicing, for literally *hours* a day, on the very devices and applications that govern our workplaces and home lives.

Society tells us that we should be scared—very scared—of this Millennial. I, for one, don't think it's that serious. Remember in Chapter 2 when I discussed the Techie? Well, this "unengaged tech addict," is just getting a bad rap. We all—educators, marketers, and parents—have to get better at communicating with Millennials. We may not speak the same language, but we can learn. Do you know that *women over the age of 50* are fastest-growing group of Facebook users? I can't tell you how many grandmothers and grandfathers are popping up on Facebook to view pictures "from my granddaughter's wedding" or to see videos of "my grandson's birth." There is always a natural inclination to fear what we don't know. The goal of this chapter hasn't been to scare you, to get you to disconnect every computer in your home, or to confiscate every cell phone. That would never work. We have opened Pandora's digital box, but what's in it shouldn't scare you; it should challenge you and enlighten you. Technology allows us to exchange thoughts and ideas in a global way. It's exciting and enlightening. Technology is like a big, deep ocean, and you have to dive in and figure out how to navigate. If you do, I promise you that you will find a way to engage with Millennials, and it will be worth it.

TINA'S TOP FIVE

1. *Technology is a way of life that provides more solutions than problems.* As our way of life begins to realize infinite technological possibilities, new problems arise every day—while older problems linger or morph into a larger set of issues that we all face. However, we can combine two basic components to solve nearly any problem we face: knowledge and skill. As shown in various examples in this chapter, the gadget-crazy youth who dominate the digital communication lines are exchanging and absorbing

(continued)

(*continued*)

information from each other at alarming rates. The growth of our knowledge base correlates to the amount we communicate. This knowledge base, combined with highly skilled people (maybe the quiet introverted techies who develop new algorithms and formulas and who are passionate about working on the very problems they've been discussing with their peers for most of their lives), results in a winning situation. Technology's endless advances and upgrades provide the foundation for developing a generation of the best problem solvers in history.

2. *Technology is an interesting dichotomy: It unites and destroys.* Sometimes, we talk too much—or listen to the wrong things. We all get overwhelmed at times in our attempts to merely keep up with what we perceive as normal daily lives. There's a lot to do, and computers seem to make our to-do lists grow longer and wider. We should probably face the fact that we'll never be able to keep up with machines that are designed to do our work for us—and to do it more precisely.

Some people get lost in the clutter. We find it harder to keep up with our schedules and the people in our lives. As life becomes less simple, we may find ourselves detached from the comforts of the things that helped us once find a common bond.

I've clearly argued that the benefits of technology outweigh the costs. Increased availability of information—combined with real-time ways to share it—brings people together who want to be in the same place and allows them to address the same issues. But I *do* acknowledge that the more we use technology, the more distracting things may become at times. There are undoubtedly times when it's necessary to turn off our cell phones, computers, TVs, and other tech devices—and actually handle things face-to-face.

3. *Technology is a threat to traditional media only because it's seen as an add-on, not an integrator.* We all know that major media outlets are starting to get swallowed up by social networking

and "word of mouth on steroids" capabilities of digital communication and content distribution. Some people argue that the music industry is dying, as is the print publishing industry (a little more slowly). Even television is becoming more fragmented. Last year, movie and television actor Ashton Kutcher gained 1 million Twitter followers faster than anyone else. The runner-up? CNN. That's right, an actor and television producer had 1 million people listening to his opinions before one of the largest news organizations on earth did.

The point here is simple: Any company that is seriously doing business *must have* some kind of an online presence—at minimum, a web site and contact page. Most companies have become their very own media outlets, vying for presence in the mass media and PR marketplace. Traditional media outlets have to play catch-up and develop strategies to *revolve* around the digital platform. The longer they wait, the more these "independent media companies" will create their own presence and continuously decrease the need for traditional media.

The one advantage that traditional outlets do still have is brand recognition. Therefore, they must leverage their audience's familiarity with their brand by providing digital offerings that can compete with the digital market rather than with the overall media market. To date, they've been asleep at the wheel, since most still view technology as an add-on to existing information. They must instead begin to focus completely on digital integration and let more antiquated models find their place in the media landscape.

4. *Technology drives global mobiles, creating a generation of young people who will work together in both positive and negative ways.* Another variable of widespread technology use among young people is the effect of technology's collaborative tools on world travel. In essence, the world is smaller than ever these days. Some people commute to work on planes, and traveling from one country to another is no longer a major event. Participation
(continued)

(*continued*)

in study-abroad programs continues to rise, and it's no longer restricted to the school year. According to a recent study by Studyabroad.com, the summer of 2010 saw the biggest increase in summer programs ever, with 44 percent of respondents saying they would want to do a summer program in the future.

This new generation of global mobiles is a walking enterprise that is interacting on projects and collaborating to build a strong knowledge base. This creates immense opportunities (and not just for travel companies) for cross-promotion and marketing that is focused on getting the attention of young globe-trotters who are enthusiastic, inquisitive, and likely to speak multiple languages proficiently.

5. *Technology has birthed a generation that is forever optimistic, always looking to innovation for a solution, never accepting defeat.* My final point about technology and its impact on young people has to do with attitude. Because they create devices and machines that seem to accomplish the impossible, technology companies are often idolized by young people. They are doing something cool and helping us all with their innovations, at the same time.

Companies and their advocates have introduced an attitude of optimism and a viewpoint of infinite possibility into our culture, particularly in younger people. When nothing seems impossible, there is less fear to give something new a try and tackle even the largest of problems.

This final point gives me confidence that the positives of technical integration outweigh the negatives. Although some days are filled with clutter (for all of us), we are surrounded by new tools every day that, with the right combination of knowledge and skill, will push us to achieve things greater than we can imagine today. They underscore the notion that, indeed, *nothing* is impossible.

Answer: False. In our spring 2010 teen survey, 62 percent of 16- to 24-year-olds did not want an iPad.

5

"Awesome!"

Everything Old School Is New Again: Why Some Brands Will Be Around When Millennials Have Kids of Their Own

BUZZSPOTTER PROFILE

"Jill, breakfast—now!," her mom yells. Ugh. Jill, 16, is trying to figure out what to wear to school. She quickly settles on a pair of classic Levi's, topped off with an "I love Coke" Junk Food T-shirt and classic Converse sneakers. She grabs her new school bag—a vintage hobo she scored at the local thrift store for $5—and heads out the door.

 Pop Quiz

True or False: One of the top five books tweens love to read is *Ramona Quimby, Age 8*.

Tweens and teens have an undeniable impact on trends in popular culture and on the brands behind these trends. For example, vampires have always lurked in the dark, but Stephanie Myers's Twilight series brought them into the daylight. The last book in the series, *Breaking Dawn*, sold 1.5 million copies in its first 24 hours on sale, and the film version of *Twilight* set box office records with an opening weekend gross of $70 million. As far as the audience for its spellbinding and lucrative predecessor, *Harry Potter*, the average age of both book buyers and moviegoers was . . . well, *young*.

It's no secret that trends change along with the times. Less than 10 percent of all U.S. ski resorts allowed a newish hybrid sport called *snowboarding* in the early 1980s; today, it's the fastest-growing winter sport in the country, thanks largely to its popularity among kids. Texting would not make up such a major part of the wireless industry were it not for teens (and parents would add that car insurance premiums would be a lot lower were it not for 17-year-old male drivers). Hip-hop artists really owe a portion of their royalties to 11-year-olds from L.A. to D.C (famous tween blogger Tavi Gevinson is a major fan).

Pop trends have historically been set by young people. Yet today's Millennials—who can change channels (and web sites) faster than any generation to date—have earned a reputation for being especially fickle. They're known for moving on to the next new thing almost as soon as the old one, be it a brand of jeans, a teen idol, or the kind of party favor in the goody bag, takes hold. Adding to this illusion is an erroneous belief that took hold (prerecession) that these kids have unlimited allowances to go along with their limited attention spans.

We all too frequently see a knee-jerk reaction from marketers to change their product, service, or message in order to keep pace with what's new. Sure, it's crucial to stay current (and therefore in business), but we can't overlook the real force behind the trends, the magic ingredient that turns fads into classics. It's a little old-fashioned something called *staying power*, and when an item is well-crafted, well-priced, and easily updated, it sticks around for more than one season. It may even be handed down to the next generation, since parents jump on board when it passes the hand-me-down test.

It seems as though people are in an almost permanent state of reflection these days. Whether they're thinking back to times that were more financially secure or less stressful (or a little of both), we're entering a period during which people want to reminisce. Can you blame them? It's only human nature to focus on a time or place that made you feel safe and comfortable. It's called *nostalgia*. Brands that may have been brushed off as nostalgic have been making major comebacks in 2010. Whether it's because technology is making them cool again or the brands are reinventing themselves, marketers can learn lessons from these products and services.

Sometimes being retro is the inspiration in and of itself. Companies like Junk Food (inspired by classic advertisements) and vintage stores like What Comes Around Goes Around (beloved by renowned stylist Rachel Zoe), prove that it's cool to be retro. Even tween style blogger and guru Gevinson loves a good thrift store.

Spotlight: Junk Food Clothing

Founded in 1998 by designers Natalie Grof and Blaine Halvorson, Junk Food Clothing has garnered international attention for its soft cotton T-shirts and casual clothing. Made famous by T-shirts emblazoned with retro logos for brands like Crush soda and Fun Dip candy, Junk Food now boasts a collection that includes designs for the NBA and NFL, as well as a partnership with Gap Kids. With fans like Sandra Bullock, Beyonce, and Paris Hilton, the brand also enjoys a loyal celebrity following. The brand found success in building from a line of retro designs, but it has been able to transition into original collections. For tweens and young teens, these tees offer an interaction with brands they may love today, but have not yet had a chance to experience in a retro or vintage form.

Reinvention

A variety of factors give a brand staying power, and the youth market has a hand in amplifying each one of them. One of the most important factors is the ability for a brand to reinvent itself.

The key to this trend is being able to merge old strengths with new ideas. It requires the ability to help customers see the same old product in a completely different light—and who better to view things from a different angle than the youth market that is likely embracing a product line for the first time? Young consumers will often recognize the classic elements of a brand (such as Converse All Stars), but will naturally offer their opinions on ways to adapt the product line to meet with their current tastes, via simple tweaks such as new color schemes and using different types of materials. Millennials are going to offer these opinions regardless, and will share them among themselves. Therefore, it's the brand's job to *listen* and engage with them where they are conversing: online and at the point of purchase. Many brands make the common mistake of refusing to listen to youth feedback;

they instead stick to what they know and refuse to reinvent. Young people are rarely asking you to adopt a completely new way of doing business; they're simply asking for a few adjustments here and there that will help upgrade their experience.

One brand that I keep referring to is Coca-Cola; however, here's an example regarding a misstep it made. Once the company decided that Facebook was becoming a big enough dot on its marketing radar, it decided to create a page to target global fans. Enter major problem: A Coca-Cola fan page already existed, and the corporation did not own it. The page is managed by two average guys named Dusty and Michael, who went looking for a Coke fan page one day and, on finding none, decided to launch their own.

Coca-Cola had to get in touch with Dusty and Michael to get its page back. Once it did, the company made another misstep. Instead of engaging with fans via Facebook the way users had become accustomed to, Coca-Cola took on a much more corporate approach. Like most companies that spend billions of dollars on a well-edited brand image, Coca-Cola had reservations about letting users have control over content—or even letting them submit original thoughts to its corporate page. As a result, the page was just not working. So the company did what it does best—reinvented its page and amped up its interaction with consumers. While it still uses its page as a place to showcase products and talk about the brand, the site feels more like a destination for fans than a corporate web site. The new approach appears to be working, as Coca-Cola has more than 21.8 million Facebook fans.

Even when their core products remain the same, brands will reinvent themselves in a variety of ways: conveying fresh marketing campaign messages, attaching to causes to adapt to certain political themes, and starting secondary product lines that act as supplements (rather than substitutes) to the core product. Entertainers who enjoy decades-long (and even longer) careers in the music industry understand this concept all too well. Michael Jackson, for example, was able to prolong his music career by constantly re-creating his image instead of relying solely on his talent to carry his success over time. He adapted his music style by incorporating the rhythms and sounds of different producers; he wrote songs that were meaningful the world over, such as "We Are The World" and "Black and White," and that allowed the theme behind the music to keep his music in the limelight; and finally, he always incorporated new elements into his stage performances that kept stadiums full and audiences interested. By using reinvention, Jackson transcended from being a great entertainer into becoming a global brand.

There are, of course, numerous examples of reinvention gone wrong. In Chapter 6, we discuss how quickly Millennials are growing up and ponder whether they *really* want to mature so fast. I personally don't believe that the majority of Millennials want to develop at warp speed; however, it certainly seems like their role models want to. The funny thing is, when has it ever been profitable for these celebrities, who are brands unto themselves, to turn from good to bad? For example, the leader of the pack, Queen Bee Britney Spears, started off as an innocent girl from Louisiana. She clued us in to the fact that she wasn't so innocent with her hit song "Oops! . . . I Did It Again" and was obviously reluctant to admit to a sexual relationship with fellow pop star Justin Timberlake. It wasn't until Britney's very own reality show (*Britney and Kevin: Chaotic*, 2004) aired that the world saw how quickly she was unraveling. Her crowning moment came in 2007, when she publicly shaved her head. Until this moment, we hadn't witnessed a star losing it right in front of our eyes. However, like any good brand, Britney Spears reinvented herself. Since her meltdown, Spears has released a slew of hits, including *Circus* and *Womanizer.* This is what happens when a brand is built out of raw talent and value. Britney Spears was able to rebound nicely because, at the end of the day, she's talented. All she had to do to reinvent herself was to focus the attention away from her personal life and back on her talent. By reverting to the talented entertainer her fans love, she has been able to whip her brand back into shape. Of course, some critics weren't so sure she could bounce back, but several hits later (and no more shaving incidents), she's managed to prove them wrong. She may not be the best singer, but she is a fairly flawless dancer and entertainer. There are so many entertainers who have star quality and star power yet lack talent. When it comes to both celebrities and brands that have lost their way, it's their sheer talent—or quality—that grants them another chance.

Next, we have Christina Aguilera. I personally don't think that she was ever squeaky-clean, but apparently many people did. When she released the appropriately titled "Dirrty," I found it interesting that so many people were up in arms. Unlike Spears, who's returned to critical acclaim (and sales), Aguilera has not really been able to cash in on her tawdry image. For a while, she seemed to disappear from the public eye. She got married, had a baby, and seemed to be a bit more settled. She recently announced her divorce, and it's been speculated that she felt that getting married derailed her career. I doubt marriage had anything to do with it. People grew tired of her product, and she was unable to reinvent herself in an original way. Who would she be this time? A genie in a bottle? A buttless chap-wearing sexpot? A Marilyn Monroe wannabe? Christina Aguilera may have an amazing voice, but original she has never been. When it comes to brands with staying power, originality is of the utmost importance.

Finally, let's look at the latest actress to hitch a ride on the bad girl express: Lea Michele Sarfati, commonly known as just Lea Michele. Sarfati started her career as a singer on Broadway. She is the break-out star of the Fox hit *Glee*, in which she plays a star singer in her high school glee club. Things seemed to be going well for Sarfati. She's been nominated for an Emmy and Golden Globe Award, and she is definitely a red carpet star. But she recently ruffled some feathers when she appeared on the cover of *GQ* magazine with two costars. The photos insinuate a threesome, and Sarfati has a few solo pictures that sparked a lot of controversy. Indeed, *New York Times Magazine* said that the cover stars were "tapping into their inner tramps."

I know these are examples of celebrity brands, but in the modern, Millennial world, celebrities and brands are one and the same. They produce products, have loyal fans, marketing campaigns, and products in stores. The only difference is, they're real people. These celebrity brands mean a lot to Millennials, and we can learn a lot from the positive and negative things that they do.

There are unspoken rules when it comes to reinvention, and like them or not, marketers need to be aware of these. Consider the difference in a brand and a "good" product or business. There are plenty of successful businesses that promote their products and services broadly and return a healthy profit for doing so. But the key to becoming a brand—rather than just another product or entertainer—is that the sense of customer loyalty develops that is so strong that customers will stick by you as you grow. For example, it's important to remember that Michael Jackson was able to maintain his brand as King of Pop and number one entertainer on the planet despite well-documented and widely broadcast periods of personal adversity. He was able to maintain staying power, at least in part, because he always wrote new songs that were relevant to the times and continuously upgraded the value of his concert performances, employing special effects and new video technologies and working with the best musical directors available to give audiences something they had never experienced before. Even today's Millennials, many of whom never saw Jackson perform during his heyday, recognize the value of his brand because they understand its global impact.

The same is true with large corporations. Even before its Facebook page blunder, Coca-Cola had a major gaffe in 1985, when it decided to replace its original cola with "new Coke." To be clear, the product was not launched with any separate name of its own—it was simply known as the new formula of traditional Coca-Cola. As you might imagine (or recall), the American public did not react well to this new beverage. They weren't even clear about what was new or what had changed. The brand was finally renamed Coca-Cola II in 1992, seven years after the damage was done. One would assume that a name as big and powerful as Coca-Cola would launch a massive marketing campaign in support of its new effort, right? Not so. The product was announced at a press conference at New York City's Lincoln Center. Many speculated that Pepsi, fearful of losing gains to Coke, fed reporters questions before the press conference. The general opinion was that Coke was changing, trying to be sweeter, like Pepsi. This was problematic, since ads featuring Bill Cosby touted Coke's "less sweet" taste as a reason to drink it instead of Pepsi. Regardless, in an article written about this event, author Blair Matthews states, "The early publicity that New Coke received was mixed—but largely favorable. More than 80 percent of the U.S. population was aware of the new formula within days of the announcement."[1]

Even though they were aware, the backlash was unbelievable. Even more stunning is the fact that the majority of consumers actually preferred new Coke in blind taste tests. However, they were loyal to "old Coke," which became known as Coca-Cola Classic and then just Coke. Coca-Coca II is still available to local distributors, and it actually sells in random foreign markets like American Samoa. Since the new Coke fiasco, Coca-Cola has introduced a variety of new beverages, including C2, Coca-Cola Zero, Diet Coke Plus, and countless others. No matter what, Coke will always survive, because it's built a loyal consumer base that trusts the brand enough to forgive mistakes. The product is also always consistently good—something that truly matters when you're aiming for longevity.

Spot-on Marketing

Another major contributor to brand staying power is spot-on marketing campaigns, which keep the brand relevant with younger customers. The key to these promotions is to create a lifestyle experience for customers rather than to just display and provide basic information about the product. One of the best examples of a brand that continues to thrive due to spot-on marketing campaigns is Nike. Who can forget the debut of its 1988 campaign, "Just Do It," via agency Wieden + Kennedy? *Advertising Age* magazine voted it one of the top five advertising campaigns of the century. Nike understands the psychological need for consumers to feel better about themselves by purchasing a product or service—and its products are inspiring. Whether it's a commercial featuring a series of famous runners and everyday people or simply flashing "Just Do It" across the screen, Nike motivates people. And when the rare blunder occurs (e.g., Nike's commercial featuring LeBron James slaying a martial arts master, which offended Chinese authorities), Nike is quick to recover.

A newer (compared to decades-old classics like Converse and Coca-Cola) emerging brand is Apple. What initially distinguished Apple from its competitors was the company's willingness to reinvent itself. It went from creating sleek-looking computers to focusing heavily on devices such as the iPod and iPhone and online marketplaces like iTunes and app stores. Yet Apple still acted based on its core principles of unprecedented product design and user experience to develop these newer ideas. These products didn't just sell themselves; they benefited from decidedly meaningful marketing and advertising campaigns that created a brand experience. Apple encouraged us all to "Think Differently," a motto that became an overall theme for its brand and product offerings. Apple then showed us images of people using its products (e.g., a graphical rendition of rapper Eminem spinning around and dancing with his iPod), thereby bringing that product into the mainstream. And of course, let's not overlook the now-legendary "Mac vs. PC" campaign. How often do we chat about defining ourselves based on what kind of computer we use? I'm sure we can all conjure up an image of someone who uses a Mac versus someone who's using a PC. Apple turned these devices from mere products into personality-defining attributes.

Spot-on marketing campaigns are necessary to extend a brand's staying power into the youth market, because they clearly exhibit what the experience of using a product or service is like. They also highlight the mission of the company that is presenting the product, thereby creating customer loyalty. Just because older generations know brands like Coke and Apple fairly well doesn't mean that younger customers will simply adopt them by default. In fact, these products' affiliation with older generations may initially dissuade Millennials if the marketing campaigns can't express the experience these brands provide. However, once the campaigns are able to capture the feeling behind what it's like to use the products, the youth market will align their affiliation and provide staying power.

What can you learn from brands like Nike and Apple? First, it's important to research and understand exactly *who* your consumer is. For example, let's say you "own" a certain target market but want to expand into another market. Don't assume that because it's worked for you in the past that it will automatically work with Millennials; instead, do your due diligence to get a feel for what might happen. Take clothing retailer American Eagle Outfitters, for instance, which decided that it wanted to ride the tween wave and start catering to younger Millennials. It would be safe to assume that a company that has so much experience in the Millennial market would know how to "age-down" successfully. However, instead of launching its tween-centered brand (called 77kids) full steam ahead, American Eagle began with an online boutique, which operated for two years before the company opened its first brick-and-mortar store (it plans to open seven this year).[2] By opening the online store first, American Eagle was able to gather real-time research data from actual current and potential customers. It also allowed the company to test products and styles to see what worked for younger consumers before opening up stores.

I suppose American Eagle Outfitters had learned its lesson from its failed chain Martin + Osa, which offered classic and contemporary J. Crew-esque clothing for 21- to 60-year-old shoppers. The 28-store chain, which just couldn't find it's footing, shut down in July 2010. It never really made a connection with its customers, and it happened to come along at a time when J. Crew was really "killing it" (as Millennials love to say). Speaking of J. Crew, the brand has had a major resurrection under the direction of president and executive creative director Jenna Lyons. At a time when retail is down 70 percent across the board, J. Crew is actually up 14 percent. With fans like Michelle Obama, the brand and its designer have developed a massive cult following.

J. Crew also teaches us that timing is of the essence when it comes to a relaunch. The brand, a pioneer of affordable luxury, really hit its stride in 2007, right before the recession hit. Since the average item costs around $80, customers can pick up a silk blouse or even a pair of nice suit pants without having to drop too much cash. However, J. Crew is currently getting into the business of serious luxury, featuring coats on its web site for as much as $1,200—one model of which sold out instantly in fall 2010. Apparently, women who can no longer afford to shop at Neiman Marcus have found their way to J. Crew.

Finally, these brands emphasize the fact that classics do matter. Nothing is quite like that classic pair of Levi's, our first Converse sneakers, or our first sip of Coke. Not much has really changed as far as these brands go. Sure, there are tons of new additions to the product families, but most of us can remember—and cherish—at least one experience with the original. These brands understand that it's important to retain current customers while expanding their base. Even the best brands have faltered from time to time; yet somehow, they find a way to reconnect with consumers and introduce them to their new experience. Companies like J. Crew do it through the power of print, with a catalog that's as much a coveted style bible as it is a sales tool for the brand. J. Crew understands and acts upon an extremely important guideline: You have to think of how you can make your marketing tools work for you.

Integration: Brand Experience

Another major factor in what makes some brands tick and others trail off for tweens and teens is the all-important brand experience. Lego, for instance, isn't just about building objects with colored, plastic minibricks—it's Lego Rock Band for the Nintendo DS; it's Sponge Bob Lego (or Star Wars Lego or Ben 10 Lego or Indiana Jones Lego); it's a family trip to Lego Land, or playing games on the visually pleasing Lego web site, or even watching YouTube's Lego channel. It's an ever-unfurling experience that can capture a child's attention and hold it into early adolescence—and it starts with the simple and satisfying act of playing with Legos on the living room floor.

Brand experience used to be an optional, added boost to marketing. Nowadays, it's an essential part of surviving in a new economy and something that this new generation of consumers expects. This approach, which can also be translated as brand extension, requires brands to take a core product that has reached a measurable level of recognition and strategically branch out to related areas that increase the experience that their products and services provide. This is one of the more nimble areas of staying power, and not every brand figures out how to execute it well. It takes a lot of time and certain amount of risk to roll out new product lines and position them successfully—while being careful not to damage the core brand's strength.

The overall objective behind brand extension, other than to produce great new product lines that can eventually flourish on their own, is to engage customers on multiple platforms and to reach them exactly where they are expecting the brand to be. A Millennial might muse that "Lego should really make a video game out of this concept" long before Lego decides to do so on its own. By actually following through and extending the brand to this area, the company shows customers that it understands their needs—and therefore is able to gain their loyalty.

Let's revisit Apple for a moment to see another great example of brand extension. As a fairly secretive organization that doesn't hint much about its next moves until they are imminent (which of course works in its favor to heighten expectations), Apple seems to have a great brand extension method that has plenty of staying power. The company launches new products (mostly portable technical devices) only every few years. It then spends the interim time adding a variety of products to existing lines and using them as a test market for new lines. For example, when Apple simultaneously launched the iPod and iTunes, it immediately started to analyze how consumers were using the product and came up with two conclusions: (1) There was a need for different versions of the iPod, as evidenced by the introduction of the Nano, Touch, and devices with various memory capacities; and (2) there were other mobile products, such as the iPhone and (eventually) the iPad, that were suitable for Apple to pursue based on the iPod's success.

Executing brand extension strategy takes a lot of planning, timing, and the guts to put money behind new product lines that carry a double risk: failing and diluting existing product lines. Apple's approach can serve as a prime example for other brands that need to study a strategy for extending from one product line to another.

Brand augmentations can also come in the form of sponsorships. For example, male grooming product Old Spice extended its relationship with one of its targets—young African-American men—via a long-term sponsorship of basketball shoemaker And1's Mixtape Tour. The tour, which traveled to 10 U.S. cities, showcased basketball players performing moves that often drew comparisons to the Harlem Globetrotters. It was documented for a show on ESPN called *Streetball* that also featured Old Spice advertisements. While the tour was a successful partnership for Old Spice, which used the opportunity to interact with customers and distribute product samples, it actually hurt And1's core business. The reason? The tour had originally been designed to be And1's brand extension vehicle; in fact, it was now more famous than the shoes. And the mix tapes—DVD reels of players performing amazing streetball moves—were selling more copies than the shoes! It's okay to look into brand extension when you clearly understand your product and your target market and have established yourself as a major player in your space. Old Spice understood this. Apparently, And1 did not, and the brand suffered because of it.

One reason might have been the departure of original And1 founders Seth Berger, Jay Coen Gilbert, and Tom Austin, three friends who attended the University of Pennsylvania's Wharton School of Business together. Since their exodus at the height of the brand's popularity, it's been sold multiple times, and it has not turned into the athletic powerhouse it had originally aimed to be.

Another frequently occurring phenomenon is celebrities acting as brand extensions. Singer/actress turned clothing designer/perfumer extraordinaire? Though that probably describes almost half of Hollywood, there's one celebrity in particular who has mastered the art of the brand extension: Gwen Stefani. She's best known as the lead singer in the rock band No Doubt, whose debut album *Tragic Kingdom*, released in 1995. More than 16 million records later, No Doubt was a monstrous success, and all eyes were on Stefani. In 2004, Stefani released her first solo album, *Love. Angel. Music. Baby*, followed two years later by *Sweet Escape*. Collectively, her solo albums have sold more than 18 million copies.

In No Doubt's early days, Stefani made most of the outfits she wore onstage, often throwing bits and pieces together to display her own funky brand of style. But by 2004, she was rocking haute couture under the fashion tutelage of stylist Andrea Lieberman. In 2004, the duo launched L.A.M.B., a clothing line featuring items that look like they're straight out of Stefani's closet. It's 100 percent genuine Gwen Stefani. She even personally sells the line at trade shows! On an episode of Bravo TV's reality docudrama *The Rachel Zoe Project*,

Zoe even visited Stefani at her booth and praised her on camera for being so personally committed to her brand.

At some point, celebrities have to realize that consumers can tell the difference between those who will happily slap their name on anything and everything and those who are truly committed to the process. It might also have something to do with a superpowerful management team or firm working backroom magic as well. It's been widely reported that Britney Spear's undoing came only after she parted ways with personal manager Larry Rudolph, whom she famously fired and then rehired to get her career on track.

If you're a marketer whose brand is flailing, you might want to pick up the phone and call a top industry manager—*not* an ad agency—to see whether he or she can help you get back on track. If a manager can pull the latest pop artist out of the gutter (sometimes literally), reinventing your brand may be easy in comparison.

Marketing Moment: You must realize that the brand experience doesn't stop with your main product. Millennials want to live your brand, and you need to be wherever they are.

Digital Engagement

A final factor in building staying power with the Millennial market is to engage them where they spend most of their time—on mobile devices and the Internet. Millennials are finicky about where they get their information; if they don't find out about your new product line until they see it on the shelf, then they'll be less likely to trust it. They'd much rather read about it on Facebook or see a #hashtag topic on Twitter that talks about your product's unveiling—*then* they'll check it out.

Major brands (and small ones, too, for that matter) are starting to create internal teams to maintain social networking sites and continuously update Twitter feeds with information on upcoming products and launch events. These pseudotechnical teams are taking the place of traditional public relations agencies and staff. Some companies are even bringing on "full-time focus groups" in the form of Millennial-aged interns who are responsible for constantly using their web sites and giving feedback for improvement for both small issues, such as web site layout and design, and larger matters, such as which product lines to launch next.

These new research and communications strategies create teams of Millennial brand ambassadors who work in the area they know best: using digital tools to convert marketing into sales. Whether they're online or just hanging out with their friends, they become walking advertisements who can explain certain products' advantages over others. Since they're actively using these products, they're also building their credibility.

Finally, there is a bottom line to brand extension and experience: *Quality counts*. Whether you're selling music or soft drinks, you can't fool a kid with something that looks okay on the outside but doesn't perform. And you definitely can't fool the parent who pays the bills—particularly in our postrecession recovery. Even the most creative and interesting advertising is ineffective if you don't research and carefully plan the product lines, not to mention that designing new items that don't fit with the core product dilute the brand and hurt customer loyalty. Though there are potentially rewarding returns, brand extension can be a risky game. Nothing replaces the ability to develop spot-on advertising that highlights reinvention via internal feedback teams and effective brand ambassadors. This approach will always be successful as long as it focuses on the key to winning new customers and keeping old ones over time: making customers *feel* what the brand really stands for, as they do every time they hear a Michael Jackson song or take a sip of Coke.

Chapter 4 discussed what technology means to today's teens and that it's crucial to engage with them digitally. One way that classic brands like Armani Exchange are connecting with Millennials digitally is through technology called Clikthrough. This tool allows users who are watching videos to literally click on images and immediately get more information on products and purchase them. It's one-click (or "one-clik") shopping, and it's the future of retail.

Even a 30-year-old brand like Armani Exchange recognizes the importance of connecting with Millennial consumers in a new and exciting way. When brands can figure out how to connect, it works. Armani Exchange's Clikthrough campaign has a 225 percent rate for hot spot clicks. Very hot indeed.

Spotlight: Clikthrough

Clikthrough was conceived in 2000, when founder Abe McCallum was watching an episode of *Friends*. He was in the middle of decorating his new apartment and was admiring a lamp on the show's famous set. He thought, "Nice lamp. I'd buy it right now if I knew what brand it was." Though it was a Eureka moment, it took McCallum almost eight years to bring his idea to fruition. He ended up developing the software he wanted, and now Clikthrough is the go-to partner for brands like Calvin Klein Jeans and Armani Exchange and magazines like *Elle*.

What lessons can we learn from brands that have stood the test of time when it comes to creating longevity with the Millennial customer? First, keep it simple. I talked earlier about brands that are able to maintain and extend their brands starting with one simple product or idea. Don't try to do too much too soon. Even celebrities—who dream of multihyphenated descriptions after their names—start out by doing just one thing. Someone who ends up as a singer-actress-designer probably started out a singer. Start simply, build a core, loyal following, and then expand based on what your fans want and seek from your brand. And remember to tread lightly. There are several examples of brand extensions outshining the very brands that created them. Remember what happened to And1? Remember how *Teen Vogue* started to cannibalize *Vogue*'s younger readership? It's a slippery slope, so be careful.

Second, don't ignore your core's emotional connection to your brand. Consumers rejected new Coke automatically; it was in no way connected to how they actually felt about this new product. How you handle your brand's messaging and communicate with your consumers is of the utmost importance. Once you establish that relationship, it goes both ways. You have to listen to your customers. They know what they want from a brand experience, and they will continue to tell you. Create unique ways to interact with them. Starbucks offers random surveys whereby customers can win free cups of coffee for going online and detailing their experience. It's a small gesture, but it goes a long way.

Finally, you can never ignore the importance of quality, whether we're talking about celebrity talent or a pair of jeans. And every brand is held to a totally different standard. For example, I doubt that people go to Forever 21 clothing stores expecting high quality; rather, they're merely looking for fast fashion at cheap prices. They know that the clothes will most likely fall apart after a few wears, but it doesn't matter to them. It's a cheap investment, and they're getting the instant gratification they crave. Luxury labels, and even brands like J. Crew, are not afforded that luxury (no pun intended!). They have to perform all the time, no matter what. You must realize that maintaining quality is sometimes all you need to do to succeed. Just look at the sleeper success of Canadian clothing brand Club Monaco. It doesn't do flashy ad campaigns, yet it's maintained a loyal following based on quality products alone.

Spotlight: Club Monaco

Founded in 1985 by Joe Mimran and Alfred Sung, Club Monaco opened its doors on popular Queen Street in Toronto, Ontario, inspiring minimalists everywhere. The first store emerged in the United States four years later, in Santa Monica, California. Although Polo Ralph Lauren acquired the brand in 1999, it has been able to continue to operate independently. Known for its mostly black-and-white collections with seasonal splashes of color, Club Monaco is the place to head for everyday basics.

There's just one final caveat that we have to discuss when we talk about keeping brands fresh and current: something called "authenticitude." This term, coined by teen research company Teenage Research Unlimited (TRU), is the notion that Millennials are more interested in the *idea* of an authentic experience than they are in the experience. A great example of this is clothing company Hollister. Even though Abercrombie & Fitch launched the brand in 2000, its products have "1893" written all over them, causing one to assume that the company was founded in 1893, right? Nope. But it doesn't matter to consumers, because Hollister has *authenticitude*. Since the brand *feels* like it was created in the 1890s, it seems totally authentic, which is all that matters.

Reality shows are also in this lane. Let's take, for example, a show (or franchise, really) like *Real Housewives of.* . . . Does it matter that these programs feature some women who aren't even wives, who are losing their houses left and right, and who can barely be described as "real"? Not really. If they're doing things we assume housewives do on TV (shopping, hosting great dinner parties, getting into hair-pulling screaming matches with other women), then it seems to work for viewers. If it's close enough to what we *think* is an authentic message, that's all that really matters.

While this seems like bad news for brands that put millions (or billions) toward creating authentic experiences, it's important to keep in mind that companies like Hollister invest a lot of money in creating these mock "authentic" brand experiences, too. At the end of the day, it's really up to consumers to decide just how real their experiences need to be. Does it matter to them if a brand was created in 1893? Not if it's not relevant in their lives today. Authenticity and heritage can take you only so far. Consumers live in the here and now, and those experiences are what really count. Remain mindful of what you can do tomorrow to continue your connection with your consumer. If you begin each day with one question—"How can I connect with my consumer?"—you will always be a better marketer in the end.

I can't express enthusiastically enough that *marketing matters* to Millennials. I am sure that there are some marketers who remember the days of marketing to Generation X—the group that loathed marketing. But it's a new day, and you have to abandon all of your preconceived notions. Each generation brings its own challenges with it. If you're looking through your archives for a bit of inspiration, remember that today's customer is not yesterday's customer, even if you're updating yesterday's product. Creating and maintaining quality brands takes time; it's not something you can do overnight. If it took 30, 50, or even 100 years to develop it, it will clearly take a lot of effort to maintain it. With every new generation of consumers come new notions of success, new demands, and new ideas for products and services. It's your job as the marketer to figure out how to communicate those brand ideas to a larger audience.

BUZZFLASH: SILLY BANDZ? SILLY CONCEPT? NO WAY!

Who knew that inexpensive colored rubber bands shaped like cats, dinosaurs, milkshakes, guitars, and trucks would become one of the hottest collectibles among today's tweens (and even some teens)? This trend probably even caught the people at Silly Bandz, the Ohio-based toy company that claims to have invented the bands, by surprise. (There are now several companies marketing the bands.) Kids collect them by the gross, wear them on their wrists, trade them at school (they've even been banned from some classrooms because teachers claim that they're a distraction), and love to hit toy stores to track down favorite or unusual styles. Sort of reminds you of those slap bracelets from the 1990s! Perhaps one reason to explain their popularity is price point: A parent can get in and out of the store with these coveted items for about $3, a cost that is also consistent with the amount of pocket change some kids may have on hand or in their piggy banks. Forget the $200 handheld gaming device—sometimes a kid just wants something low-tech . . . and fun. After all, hula hoops and Frisbees still sell.

TINA'S TOP 5

1. *Brand experience is the single most important factor for today's Millennials.* It's all about *feeling* for this generation. In a world where every product has numerous competitors and plenty of varieties from which to choose, the successful products and services must highlight the intangible value that they provide. This goes hand in hand with fulfilling their brand's mission, the purpose behind creating the products they create (and for whom), and focusing on what it *feels* like when a commercial airs or a customer uses their product.

2. *Keep it simple. Some of the most important brands of our time are simple ideas.* Simplicity is absolutely crucial, especially now, in a world that moves at such a frenetic pace. Frankly, if I can't describe what your product does in a few sentences (or less than 140 characters on Twitter), the word of mouth it gets is going to be extremely slow or nonexistent. The majority of customers—young people included—are looking for ideas that work (quality) and are extremely effective in their niche (simplicity). For example, Apple successfully transitioned from focusing on home computers to developing portable personal devices based on the simple notion that people want to take all their music with them wherever they go, without having to lug around CDs. After Apple created the iPod— and not before—it then took the liberty to go into other areas, such as mobile communication and touch-screen Web browsing.

3. *Quality has always been, and will continue to be, a key element to success with Millennials.* No matter how cool an idea is or how great a product looks, quality matters to Millennials above all else. Remember, this generation is growing up in the worst economic downturn in the past 80 years. They aren't going to frivolously spend their dollars on something that they won't be able to use repeatedly. They become frustrated when they have to return something that doesn't work, and they voice their opinions on inferior quality through a variety of mediums: in person, via word

of mouth, through Facebook comments, by Twitter blasts, and in mass text messages and e-mails to friends, family, and whoever else will listen. It's vital for brands seeking staying power (in short, all of them) to uphold quality when attempting brand extension.

4. *Brand extensions are a necessary part of marketing to Millennials.* You have to set yourself apart; diversity is king. We're well past the days of having a great product and spending a boatload of money on marketing the same message so many times that people are simply expected to go out and purchase it. Brands have to find a way to get their products (or related product lines) in front of people wherever possible. *Harry Potter* started as a fascinating book and has since branched out into movies, toys, and action theme parks. The brand focused on the *experience*, which is exactly what brand extension provides. The story was certainly captivating enough to sell millions of books, but the subsequent titles in the series wouldn't have been so successful if it weren't for the market share provided by the movies and toys.

5. *Don't hesitate to look for inspiration in the archives.* Brands that have been around for a while have an advantage: They're able to revisit their old catalogs from time to time and see what products they might be able to reintroduce or reinvent. Nike, for example, has done an excellent job of doing retro releases of some of their classic shoes, such as the Air Force Ones and all of the Jordan series sneakers. Not surprisingly, some of these product lines are even more successful than the originals (which were also quite successful in their time). This is because, for one thing, quality products will always have a place in the market, and second, Millennials are extremely interested in incorporating the old school into their modern lives.

Answer: True. The book was number 5 on our tween hot list in 2010.

6

"I Just Want to Be Mii (and Me)"

The Importance of Letting Kids Be Kids

BUZZSPOTTER PROFILE

Emma, 12, couldn't wait to hit the mall with her mom, Claire. She had been waiting all week for this shopping trip. There were several items on her list: a new outfit for her first school dance, lip gloss, new shoes. "Ok Emma, let's get to shopping!" Was she really going to follow her around the mall? "Oh, Mom, I thought I'd just look around and . . ." Emma started to say, when her mom interjected, "Oh, and I'm going to look with you. You need a lot of stuff, but we're on a budget." Looks like Mom's in control again.

 Pop Quiz

Which show has more viewers?

a. *Gossip Girl*
b. *Secret Life of the American Teenager*

You couldn't look too far in any direction over the past four years without spotting Miley Cyrus, known to children's television fans as Hannah Montana. This daughter of one-time country music sensation, Billy Ray Cyrus was *everywhere*. No doubt partially due to her father's extensive experience in the entertainment industry, Miley Cyrus was able to quickly and efficiently climb the ranks of the children's entertainment industries (television, music, and movies) in a few short years.

The strategy to launch her to kiddie stardom initially seemed flawless. Cyrus began as lovable Hannah Montana on a Disney feature show, which immediately introduced her to a widespread audience and rode the coattails of Disney's credibility with parents. This television popularity served as a vehicle to market her music (certainly keeping her close to Billy Ray's connections), which quickly developed into national tours and stadium concerts. These concerts gave her the chance to step outside the television and interact personally with fans. Combine nationwide stadium tours with merchandising and movie opportunities, and Miley Cyrus became a flying star who transcended her roles as actress and musician to become a *brand*.

It seemed perfect . . . maybe a bit too much so. This child of one of country music's most recognizable names seemed to have executed the perfect strategy to become a teen sensation across multiple entertainment mediums—all while maintaining a squeaky-clean image. Cyrus's good-girl reputation prompted a large youth fan base to relate to her, making her a safe choice for parents as well.

However, all of that changed when, in April 2008, Cyrus posed for a racy photo shoot for *Vanity Fair* magazine that was more suitable for *Maxim* readers than her own loyal fans. Almost immediately, this media darling, who up until that point had received only positive reviews that were written with delicate attention toward her pure image, became the focus of a vicious backlash by parents of her tween fans who felt betrayed and let down. Cyrus compounded the damage shortly thereafter with some particularly sexy music videos and live television performances. With Facebook commentary buzzing about her new grown-up image, the mainstream media amplified the negativity. The paparazzi took the frenzy to its peak by following her around Los Angeles and other cities for weeks, spinning photos of her neighborhood walks into clandestine rendezvous with potential beaus. In what seemed like an overnight about-face, Cyrus went from media darling to a tabloid punch line. She tried to show her "maturity" a bit too quickly by abandoning her tween-friendly image (which was true to her own age at the time); the ultimate cost to her brand is yet to be seen.

Since actors and musicians like Miley Cyrus are brands unto themselves, we can discuss this situation as we would any brand that completely and suddenly changes its image. What would happen if, for instance, Burger King decided to forgo selling burgers and instead opted to focus solely on making vegan food? It would probably lose the burger fans and pick up a new PETA-loving crew. Obviously, a brand as big as Burger King has a smart management team in place with marketing skills to make this (albeit potentially rocky and time-consuming) transition happen. Celebrity brands are the same. Miley Cyrus still has fans, which may not be the core set she started out with back in her Disney days, but she certainly still has plenty of them. The question for parents is this: How do you shield your children from the often questionable effects of a young celebrity's growing pains?

While tweens may be investing their time in these celebrity brands, their parents are investing the money—and these parents have the ultimate responsibility of protecting their children from negative influences. That's quite a tall order these days. Considering the fact that tweens are frequently more comfortable with technology than are older generations, parents sometimes feel a few steps behind. They're unsure about what to do and exactly how to do it.

Of course, the notion of these teen celebrities gone wild is not an entirely new one. We certainly can't forget the original bad girl— Drew Barrymore. Barrymore was born to Hollywood royalty in 1975, granddaughter of legendary actor John Barrymore, and had a break-out role in the 1982 hit movie *E.T.: The Extra-Terrestrial*. The film's unbelievable success made Drew one of the best-known child stars in Hollywood—followed by what is now a well-worn script for child stars who receive too much, too soon. Drew found herself in rehab twice, seeking help for both alcohol and substance abuse. That was all it took for Drew to clean up her act. She has since starred in numerous hit films, and also enjoys a career as an incredibly suc-cessful producer. As a Screen Actor's Guild and Golden Globe award-winning actress, Drew has transitioned from troubled child star to bona fide A-list actress as nicely as could be accomplished. But the roller-coaster beginning of her career still begs the question, does it always have to happen this way?

The stories of other actresses who started their careers at young ages—Natalie Portman, Emma Watson, and Jodie Foster come to mind—prove that the answer is no. Although I'm sure these three have a comprehensive understanding of the intricacies of child star-dom, all were able to not only avoid the pitfalls, but even end up in the Ivy League. As with most things, it's all about making the right choices, having a strong support system, and staying grounded. Portman is known for her strong family; Watson is rarely seen on red carpets; and Foster is a notoriously private star. You have to wonder if the younger stars who do find themselves off track are simply vic-tims of Wharholism, the seemingly unending quest for fame.

You also have to ask what this societal tendency shows them and us. Apparently, it is that the "badder" you are, the more fame and attention you'll receive. This is very seductive mentality with which Millennials have to contend—and it's not just the pull of fame that's at play with these child stars. They also just want to grow up and spend the millions upon millions of dollars that they earned during their childhoods. They rode the wave of stardom into adulthood so quickly that they outgrew themselves and their fans. It makes you wonder, what was their hurry? And what is the secret to the success of celebrities who have managed to get it right? Time after time, you'll hear that their parents and families play key roles in keeping them rooted in reality. Millennial celebrity or not, the lesson is clear: Your family unit is still the key to your success. This likely makes parents mentors, teachers, coaches, and marketers alike wonder, how do we toe the fine line of just letting kids be kids, while still compelling them to accept some responsibility in their lives?

There is no phrase that I loathe more than a celebrity's claim that it's "not my job to be a role model." It's an interesting declaration—and one that's become very popular as of late. Their job, as they often say, is to entertain. But who are they entertaining? After all, if you took away every tween fan from stars like Miley Cyrus and Lindsay Lohan, they would have no career. Zero. Zilch. Their careers were built on the backs of loyal tween fans and, most important, *their parents' money*. It's therefore fairly maddening to watch them endure these life transitions and hear that we're all supposed to be understanding. After all, they are totally fine with the fact that they're taking their fans' money on their path to self-discovery.

Yet more often than not, these stars are not the only ones to blame. If parents boycotted the merchandise of wayward young stars (e.g., stopped buying Miley Cyrus's CDs and movies), then these celebrities' careers would be over. However, it's a double-edged sword for parents, who don't want to disappoint their children and want to support the celebrities their kids love. But parents can make a difference. They truly have power when they unite.

Consider the uproar that countless parents made over the new, improved *Dora the Explorer* when it was announced that this children's cartoon television character was going to be aged-up to a tween.

Though Nickelodeon initially released only a shadowy sketch, parents went absolutely mad. They were livid—without even seeing much to react to! Once Nickelodeon issued the final image, it was clear that there was no wrongdoing. Dora was entirely age-appropriate and still a character most children could relate to. But one has to wonder whether that initial uproar could have killed a potentially great product.

It often seems like we live in a world of ping-pong, an ongoing game between parents and celebrities, with neither party willing to take the blame for the content kids are consuming. Yet we're all going to have to deal with the effects of an oversexualized, overstimulated generation of kids at some point. It might not be something we want to face or take the blame for, but as the saying goes, "The chickens will come home to roost."

Are the Millennial fans of teen celebs in the same huge rush to grow up as their idols? In some ways, it appears that younger generations are acquiring the trappings of adulthood at younger ages: They possess laptops and cell phones before their teens; tween girls are into miniskirts and sexy Halloween costumes; and many high schoolers already have credit cards (research states that one out of every three high school seniors has one).[*] Despite the fact that Millennials have the tools and the mind-set to engage in the adult world at an age much younger than previous generations, their lack of experience fails them when they do so.

Although many young people tend to want to grow up and experience life quickly, the media presents a skewed portrayal of this propensity as specific to the entire Millennial generation. To the contrary, there are consistent trends from the past 10 years that show that young people are in no hurry to rush into adulthood. The recession certainly plays a part in their thinking, in that dependence on parents during high school and college serves as a security blanket. Until it is ripped off like a Band-Aid once Millennials enter the

---

[*]According to JUMP$TART, a not-for-profit organization that promotes financial literacy from pre-K through college-age, one in three high school seniors has a credit card. www.jumpstart.org

workforce as young adults, this dependence protects young people from the economic realities of adulthood.

Millennials may not have surpassed their Generation X siblings when it comes to their academic achievements, but they still have plenty of time. According to a recent Pew study, 39 percent of 18- to 29-year-olds are in high school, college, grad school, or professional school. So far, 19 percent of Millennials are college graduates, and an additional 26 percent are still in school. This puts Millennials on course to overtake Gen Xers (about 50 percent of whom hold college degrees) as the most educated generation in history. Millennials are passionate about being educated; some are even deferring their careers in this bad economy. Ironically, this display of more experienced thinking protects young adults from throwing themselves into full-scale adulthood by delaying certain economic realities (self-funded living situations and loan deferment period expirations) while also building a more credible resume for the job market. Indeed, the number of people taking the Law School Admissions Test rose by 20 percent in 2009. Students opting for the Graduate Record Examination rose by 13 percent, according to test administrator Educational Testing Service. This is a staggering reversal from 2008, when, at the beginning of the recession, GRE was down by 2 percent.

Besides prolonging their education, young adults are also postponing marital commitments and giving themselves more time build a more solid economic foundation. Since the turn of the millennium, research suggests that Millennials are more reluctant to get married soon after entering into the workforce, and some seem completely comfortable with the idea of forgoing matrimony altogether. According to the U.S. Census Bureau's 2009 American Community Survey, the share of married young adults aged 25 to 34 dropped 10 percentage points (from 55 percent to 45 percent) between the years 2000 and 2009. Considering the fact that the first half of that decade was a time of unprecedented prosperity, it's safe to assume that economic conditions are not the sole cause of young adults' lack of enthusiasm for marital commitment throughout the entire decade; it's also a cultural choice. After witnessing commonly cited divorce rates of 50 percent or more for their parents' generation, young people are more reluctant to rush into this common tenet of adulthood. In fact, during the same decade, the percentage of young adults who have never been married has increased dramatically from 34 percent to 46 percent. As young adults continue to redefine adulthood, from educational decisions to romantic partnerships, research suggests that the masses of young people are much more willing to take it slowly than the teen and young adult celebrities who drive the opinions portrayed in the mainstream media.

Author Dan Kiley discusses this inclination in his book, *Peter Pan Syndrome: Men Who Have Never Grown Up.* I don't think that it's just young men who don't want to grow up. Young women love their independence, and they love the freedom to make and spend money as they please. The images in pop culture and on TV, especially, don't necessarily make you want to run down the aisle. In our current culture, it's okay to focus on yourself and be selfish. It's easy to see how an institution like marriage, which is about two people becoming one and living a life together, can be sidelined by our fascination with egomania. One of my buzzSpotters sums it up this way: "I just wanna do me."

Yet this notion of focusing solely on what *I* want and how *I* feel is wreaking havoc on our society, and I'm not talking only about its impact on institutions like marriage. It comes across in executives who are so greedy that they just want to "do *me*," and therefore they destroy thousands of employees' and investors' careers and futures. I'm also talking about consumers so enamored by celebrity lifestyles that they live above their means, financing purchases on credit cards they can no longer pay, just trying to "do me." Of course, the desire to stay single (or to get divorced) is not as simple as just wanting to "do me"; however, this attitude starts somewhere. And the more it permeates, the more deeply entrenched it becomes in our overall society and psyche.

Yet as important as it is for people of all ages to feel their independence, it is just as vital to feel a part of something bigger. Belonging to a group of some kind, whether it's a massive Preppy crowd or a few Independents, has always been crucial for creating and fostering ideas. Just think of all of the Fortune 500 companies and major tech players that were either started or maintained by families or friends—Estée Lauder, Campbell's Soup, and Twitter, to name a few. One of our greatest strengths as Americans is our ability to unite behind an idea or cause and make it as big as we can dream. It's the American Dream. You have to wonder what happens when we decide to showcase increasingly negative images of family, marriage, and working together in general.

What we appear to be currently experiencing might be described as *Peter Pan 2.0: Millennial Edition*. Instead of accelerating time and often leapfrogging years of formative experience, young adult Millennials are more content to cling to the comfort of the security blankets provided by their parents and the benefits of student life (from loans to subsidized living and eating situations). They desire both the comforts of home and the space to figure out what their next steps will be. It appears that Millennials are learning from the missteps of these celebrities by and easing their way into the limelight of adult responsibility and taking something of a mature time out.

Still, the trend on the younger side of the Millennial spectrum, specifically with tweens and early teens, is to want to accelerate quickly into adulthood. Kids and teens at these ages consider the responsibilities of adulthood to be cool; they want to be respected enough by their peers and their parents to make big decisions about their lives. Older Millennials (late teens and young adults) start to temper their aspirations for more responsibility once they get a true taste of the complexities that come along with it. Although technology and globalization have certainly spawned cultural shifts, allowing young people to get to information more quickly and therefore learn more about what life has to offer at a young age, examples of consistently poor decision making among members of this group suggest that a significant portion of wisdom develops over time, with experience. No matter the technical advances we witness, this human tendency is not likely to change.

Unfortunately, many teen stars accelerate too quickly nowadays, which forces them to learn lessons with serious adult consequences in the public eye, much to the detriment of their careers. Their exposed demise shows that younger Millennials, though constantly itching to learn quickly and cut a few corners, are not ready to give up some of the wholesome values that they hold dear. They may privately snicker and gossip about some of the more risqué subjects with their very close friends, but in public (and in front of their parents), they generally respect certain boundaries and exhibit a sense of moral values.

Brands can learn from these examples by finding the appropriate balance between the tweens and teens who crave accelerated growth from time to time and the young adults who reminisce about the more carefree days of their childhood. By simply highlighting these two ends of the spectrum, marketers can take advantage of the sentiments that come along with the paradox that results from the journey into adulthood. In other words, brands can turn to young adults—the very group influencing tweens' hurried aspirations—to show examples of how it's cool to slow down rather than rush into decisions that have major consequences. Young adults and tweens alike are growing weary of their generation being portrayed by irresponsible celebrities and starlets, along with a growing stable of reality TV shows that choose to highlight their contemporaries engaging in debauchery and silliness. The brands and networks that are promoting the party lifestyle are engaging in risky behavior that is a lot like the subjects of their shows and campaigns. Contrary to what networks think, there are plenty of young people who carry themselves with class, are ambitious, and are willing to learn the ins and outs of the adult world at a moderate pace. With tools like Facebook allowing their peer groups a peek into the details of their lives, no one truly has all that much privacy anymore. All of us—not just celebrities—could benefit from a return to clean living.

Gossip Girl Still On Air? What Gives?

Gossip Girl, a teen drama series on the CW Network, is based on salacious novels written by Cecily von Ziegesar. Created by Josh Schwartz and Stephanie Savage, the series premiered in September 2007 and is based on the lives of Manhattan's Upper East Side elite. It is narrated by an all-knowing, borderline cyberbully voiced by actress Kristen Bell. *Gossip Girl* started off with decent ratings, premiering with 3.5 million viewers.[1]

(continued)

(*continued*)

Though these were not at the level the network would have liked, the show was performing well with 18- to 34-year-olds and was renewed for a second season that premiered to 3.43 million viewers.[2] The third season premiered with 2.55 million viewers[3], and ended with a disappointing 1.98 million viewers.[4] Season four premiered to a 29 percent ratings decrease. You may well be asking yourself, how and why is a show that's consistently lost viewers each season still on the air?

It clearly has something to do with cultural saturation. That's right, *Gossip Girl* is everywhere. The show counts among its cast some of the sexiest nonteenage stars on TV. Blake Lively (current muse of *Vogue* magazine editor in chief Anna Wintour), Leighton Meester, Penn Badgley, and Chace Crawford are among the show's many twenty something stars. Maybe shows starring teenagers (or teenaged characters) aren't really that appealing? Well, that's not entirely the case, either. Just ask the stars and fans of ABC Family's *Secret Life of the American Teenager.* According to *Variety*, the show debuted to 2.83 million viewers, and its Nielsen ratings for its second season premiere rose to 4.68 million viewers. And I bet you'd be hard-pressed to name even one of the stars of this show. It's not that *Secret Life*, which deals with relationships between parents, friends (and, oh, yes, addresses the controversial issue of teen pregnancy), isn't entertaining. For some reason, it simply hasn't been able to grab the pop culture attention that *Gossip Girl* has.

All of the attention is not good. *Gossip Girl* is, quite frankly, a parent's worst nightmare. Glamorized underage drinking, threesomes, and drugs—*lots* of drugs—is what you'll find in the first 20 minutes of an episode. The Parents Television Council has been very critical of the show, but all this censure seemed to bring even more attention to the series. Quotes from the council and other sources were used in an ad campaign supporting the second season, with quotes like "Mind-Blowingly Inappropriate" and "A Nasty Piece of Work." Interestingly enough, it's not like the campaign helped the ratings at all. It still begs the question: What gives—and what keeps this show on the air?

Not surprisingly, as is the case with most other areas of marketing to the Millennial generation, Mom and Dad hold the keys. Parents generally react to the types of behavior they want to prohibit by placing restrictions on their kids' habits, with a particular focus on how they consume entertainment. The same technical tools that kids are using to view content that may be more suitable for adults are tied to similar tools built into the technology to limit the kids' access. Privacy mechanisms for web sites and television channel blocking are becoming more popular and allow parents to selectively filter content before it gets to their children. But does this kind of approach really work? Can parents really outsmart their Millennial children when it comes to technology? There was a day and time when Mom and Dad had all the answers (or at least could respectably fake it). Nowadays, you see tweens showing their parents how to use fancy new cell phones (most likely a hand-me-up) and how to use services like Skype.

The parent-child relationship is a delicate balancing act these days, and I can only imagine how perplexing it must be for marketers. It's complicated, tricky, and ever-evolving. But to master it, at least as much as possible, is of utter importance to Millennial marketers. Where should new and emerging brands go for inspiration? I would suggest beginning by looking at how large consumer packaged goods companies like Procter & Gamble and Johnson & Johnson talk to Millennials and their parents.

Spotlight: BeingGirl.com

If you're looking for an example of a marketer who can talk to Millennials about difficult subjects, embrace their parents, and sell tons of stuff, look no further than BeingGirl.com. The web site, owned and created by Procter & Gamble, provides girls with a safe place to talk about personal body issues. Girls can "Ask Iris" anonymous questions about their most perplexing and private topics, and parents can find solace in the team of

(continued)

> (*continued*)
> medical experts who are advising their daughters. BeingGirl
> .com is also a hot spot for content; past partnerships include
> Sony Music and the *New York Times* best-seller *Cathy's Book*.

In order to weave through the complexities created by the transition from childhood to adulthood, marketers would be wise to focus on the family structure itself. As I mentioned before, older siblings who were in a rush when they were younger but are now putting on the brakes can serve as examples for their younger siblings, who might be more likely to listen to their older brothers and sisters than to their own peer groups. Of course, parents generally set the tone for the household's values and morals and must therefore always be respected.

Parents are a vital part of this equation, and not merely because they need to be respected. As I've stated so many times, parents are taking back the power of the purse as we emerge from this recession. Do they want their children to be happy? Of course. What parent doesn't? But after the recent economic climate wiped away almost all of the *wants*, and even a few of the *needs*, Millennials and their parents have emerged, happier in many ways, with less.

Families have also gotten much closer—and even though this, too, may be a result of a need versus a want, it's still happening. A recent Pew study found that 13 percent of 22- to 29-year-olds moved back in with their parents as a result of the recession, and 41 percent of teen panelists in a recent buzzSpotter survey said that they were spending more time with their families as a result of the recession. This quality time is also serving to restore balance in households.

Much has been written about the generation of parents who sent their children into the world believing that they were the best—that everyone wins and gets a trophy. It seems that Millennial parents, or at least parents of younger Millennials, are learning from the mistakes of this "Why worry?" generation of parents.

Millennials are, by and large, the children of caring parents who keep a watchful eye on the decisions their kids make and who exert a major influence on these decisions. Letting kids be kids can be a brilliant marketing strategy for some companies that want to target both kids *and* parents—and even the older siblings, some of whom are now young adults and won't object to an enjoyable Disney movie with their little brother or sister.

How can marketers safely promote their products and services to Millennials while managing to please their parents? It takes a lot of patience and planning, but it can be done. Here's a list of a few brands that have done it successfully, along with some tips that they've taught us.

1. **Cheetah Girls.** Sassy is not the same as sexy, and sass sells big-time. This property began as a series of books by Deborah Gregory and has since launched three films on the Disney Channel. Loved by millions of girls worldwide, the Cheetah Girls books are based on a group of singing girls who are trying to make it big and make all of their dreams come true. That's certainly an inspirational message parents can get behind— and tweens love the associated glamour, fame, and fortune.

2. **Smashies Organic Applesauce.** Here's a marketing lesson for everyone who's selling to tweens. We love to say that tweens love everything they shouldn't have, and the more untouchable it is, the better, right? No. Simply not true. Tweens are capable of loving good stuff, too. Smashies is an example of this, and it makes healthy eating easy for tweens by making applesauce fun to eat. First of all, the applesauce is packaged in a squeezable, resealable pouch. Second, the overall packaging is very cool (bright, colorful, and fun) and very kid-friendly. It's clear that the packaging speaks to tweens and children, not to their parents. So the communication is with tweens, not their parents. The product doesn't say, "Eat me because I'm good for you," it says, "Eat me because I'm cool."

3. **MTV's Rock the Vote.** There was a time when Millennials thought politics was boring. Now, young adults are voting in big numbers (92 percent of our voting-age buzzSpotters were planning to vote in the 2010 midterm election), and they

are much more aware of the issues. While we might credit President Obama for some of this, it actually started years ago, with MTV's Rock the Vote campaign. This network has always had a knack for pissing off parents, then teaching their children something valuable. Some brands don't necessarily need parent approval, and MTV is one of them. MTV is an advocate for Millennials—not for their parents. But parents should appreciate the network's ability to get through to their children—even when the parents can't. That's a lot of power, but then again, MTV has spent over 25 years earning that loyalty.

What can we learn from all this? Well, first, there's definitely a thin line between what's appropriate and what sells. I'm not saying that you can't be thought-provoking or do what it takes to cut through the noise. Millennials are being targeted every day by thousands of marketers who all want their dollars. It's a fight to the finish, and only the strong brands survive. The recession has only served to further separate the good marketers from the bad. I've talked about how Millennials are now having to think about "this or that," and not the usual "this and that," which means that both Millennials and their parents are scrutinizing every element of your brand. The younger contingent is wondering, "Is this product cool enough?" "Does it make a statement about who I want to be?" And they're looking to their parents to answer the most important question: "Can I afford this?" The good marketers show Millennials that they can't afford *not* to buy their wares.

Marketers must also ask themselves if they want to align with a celebrity, and the answer changes across every Millennial subset. For tweens, I would say absolutely yes, since so many of them are looking for someone to admire. As much as they are coming into their own, they are still looking for direction. However, a celebrity tie-in is less important for teens, since they're developing their own personalities, and Warholism is taking its place. Teens want the lives their favorite celebrities have. For that reason, contests like "My Grammy Moment," which offered Millennials a chance to perform live onstage with teen pop sensation Justin Timberlake, might be more up their alley than a commercial that merely features the pop star du jour.

You have to be sensitive to what these subsets are asking for and how they want you to market to them. Young adults are more focused on the importance of reflection. They want to see themselves in both the brands they love and the advertising for these brands.

Marketers also need to remember that edgy doesn't always sell. For instance, clothing company Dollhouse ran a notorious set of ads featuring model Joanna Krupa . . . topless. Who, exactly, were those ads for? Dollhouse is a juniors' line with prices rarely above $29.99. Its customers are a true juniors' customers—most likely tweens or young teens. At the same time, the brand was running ads in *Jane* magazine, a journal focused on college, that were meant to appeal to twenty something women. It's okay to have high hopes for your brand and to want to extend to another category, but you must know and accept your current customer. Sure, Dollhouse's campaign was exciting, and Krupa is gorgeous, but she's also a *Maxim* Hot 100 Model. That hardly seems appropriate for a brand targeting 14-year-old girls.

People too frequently assume that merely making noise, whether for something positive or negative, is the only way to appeal to Millennials. They also believe that, when it comes to ad campaigns, the edgier the better. Millennials have been there, done that. It's funny how obsessed the media is with a show like *Gossip Girl,* whereas Millennial viewers clearly aren't that enamored. Yet a show like *Secret Life* gets little love outside of the mainstream teen market (star Shailene Woodley has graced the covers of *Seventeen* and *Girls' Life* magazines). *Gossip Girl* reminds adults of the teen years we wish we had, complete with the glamorous lifestyle, friends—not to mention those fabulous clothes! Who wouldn't want that amazing wardrobe? However, we have to keep in mind that marketing to Millennials is about what *they* want, not about us reliving our teen fantasies.

We also have to be careful not to confuse *wants* with *needs*, as Millennials still want plenty of things that aren't needs. I'm not saying that Millennials are interested only in basic requirements, especially as we emerge from the recent recession. On the contrary, 35 percent of our buzzSpotters are shopping on a weekly basis. But 78 percent of them admit that they now think before they spend, which means that we need to put a lot of thought into our marketing messages. What benefit does your product offer a Millennial? Is there some value for parents, as well? Old Navy may be a clothing retailer, but it offers value and satisfies needs and wants. Young people want to be stylish, and they need to wear clothes; Old Navy provides fashionable clothes at reasonable prices. It's not rocket science, of course, but it works. I know that Old Navy has the brand power of Gap behind it, enabling the company to spend a lot of money marketing to Millennials; however, smaller companies can be successful, too. Just look at secondhand retail chain Plato's Closet, one of the fastest-growing retail chains in the country. The store focuses on reselling "gently worn clothes," and it's incredibly popular with teens and their parents.

There really is such a fine line between what's appropriate and what has crossed over into tasteless. We've seen what happens when we push—or merely allow—our kids to grow up too fast; it's not pretty. The major issue here is time. Millennials, and all of us, really, can never get our childhoods back; we all have to grow up, accept responsibility, and become adults at some point. We often hear that the grass is always greener on the other side, a saying that applies to Millennials. It's in their nature to want to mature and do grown-up things. But the same tweens who one minute assert their independence are looking for parental help the next. It's our job as the adults in their lives to set proper boundaries for our children—and that includes shielding them from any brand or experience that's not appropriate. There is definitely nothing cooler than growing up and remembering that you had an awesome childhood and that you enjoyed every minute of it . . . even if you were doing kiddie things.

TINA'S TOP 5

1. *Recognize that it's definitely a tightrope walk between what Millennials want to see and what is age-appropriate.* This is especially true for younger Millennials. Even as they are urged to slow down by their older siblings and parents, younger

Millennials are going to stray from time to time to experiment with entertainment and activities intended for adult audiences. This behavior has been historically consistent and should not be excessively belabored by parents lest tweens and young teens feel overly confined. The age-old rule that people want what they can't have still applies. The increased availability of risqué materials, brought on by technical advances, makes concerned parents' jobs harder than ever. The key is for both marketers and parents to understand where to draw the line regarding what is acceptable for age groups who cannot yet make their own adult decisions. However, it's a huge mistake to assume that some of more popular Millennials running around the Hollywood club scene are exemplary of the generation as a whole. Indeed, it's quite the opposite.

2. *Being edgy doesn't always equal success (refer to our case study on* Gossip Girl*).* With the explosion of options for television networks—and content creators in general—to distribute their ideas, writers everywhere are constantly generating new ideas and revamping old ones. Television, for example, offers thousands of hours of airtime on hundreds of affinity channels that must be filled with content and concepts that will hopefully keep current viewers loyal while attracting new ones. But the plethora of choices makes this increasingly difficult. A common emerging strategy is to do something risqué by following the old adage that "sex sells." An increasing number of reality television programs feature groups of young people to whom producers give free license—even encourage—to perform lewd acts and embarrass themselves. While this strategy occasionally leads to success, it often does not. For every kid who sneaks off to watch a forbidden program in his or her house without parental supervision, there are more and more young people who are becoming increasingly offended with the content and the producers' decisions to purposely egg on and air televised debauchery. And disappointed viewers generally point their anger toward the networks rather

(continued)

(continued)

than the individual programs. This can cause extensive problems for networks, which are already struggling to retain advertising market share due to the continuing rise of affinity cable networks and on-demand programming. My advice to these networks (and other content distributors) is this: Proceed with caution and engage your audience. Although the initial reactions to edgy content may seem exciting due to the boisterous noise that is initially created, ratings generally slip over time, and offensive programs can permanently damage network brand loyalty.

3. *Marketers must do a good job of giving their audience what they* want *and what they* need. In postrecession America, needs are again outranking wants. The years of excess and waste are gone, and not only are they behind us, but they're no longer tolerated. America is experiencing a huge shift toward focusing *first* on what people need and *then* (assuming there's a bit of time or money left over) including a few extras. While parents of Millennials lived most of their lives during an unprecedented period of economic prosperity, Millennials are more likely going to resort to the thinking and culture typical of their grandparents, who grew up during the Great Depression and World War II. During those times, much like the ones we're experiencing now, penny-pinching and bargain hunting was so necessary that it bred a culture of coupon cutting, bargain-basement shopping, and staying in on Friday nights to play cards instead of catching a movie. Once society commits to this way of life for an extended period of time—and the past 18 to 24 months is likely enough—this frugal way of thinking becomes not only necessary but also cool. Millennials transitioning into adulthood are bragging to their friends about the great deals they're getting instead of flaunting a new luxury item as they might have done only three or four years ago. Marketers who are used to simply focusing on kids who loosely spend their parents' disposable income will have to make some quick adjustments to catch

up with a generation that has no problem looking for sales and being choosey about how they spend their time and money on entertainment. For example, they're less likely to watch a meaningless reality TV series that shows young people wasting time and exhibiting no ambition. There's plenty of other programming available featuring young people that may carry an interesting message while at the same time educating and entertaining audiences. This combination of value and knowledge, along with the elimination of waste, is priceless to Millennials, who value time and money almost as much as the Depression-era generation.

4. *Parents, especially Moms, have regained the power of the purse.* They're watching every penny spent and are more often looking for a reason to say no than yes. It seems as though most marketers want to figure out a way to separate a mom and her Millennial when it comes to making buying decisions. Yet today more than ever, moms have a lot of power—and it's not just about the allowance they're giving to their children. Consider the money they're spending for the household overall. Family health and beauty care needs, from toothpaste to hair shampoo, all need to be purchased, and those decisions rest with moms. When we think of Millennials and their relationships with their parents and spending, most discussions seem to center around entertainment and fashion, but there are so many other purchases that need to be made to keep the household running properly. Although Millennials have a lot of influence over what eventually makes it into the shopping cart, you can't ignore moms. Bigger brands like Dove are creating materials and web sites that target moms and separate web sites that target their Millennial children.

5. *Aspiration always sells.* As this chapter describes, Millennials make a crucial transition: from forward-looking tweens who aspire to be and think like their older counterparts to backward-looking

(*continued*)

(continued)

young adults who reminisce about easier times when they're faced with the first waves of adult decision making. Plenty of old clichés still hold true: "The grass is always greener." "You always want what you can't have." For marketers, a strategy of focusing on what young people aspire to become, when properly researched, will always resonate with the target audience. For example, all tweens do not want to rapidly develop out of their younger years and take on a world of responsibility. On the contrary, they often cling to their youthfulness and the freedom it affords them, especially in regard to their time. However, they crave respect and aspire to be put into positions where their decisions carry some weight. The key is to give them a slot where they feel like they are making a contribution without overwhelming them with choices that they can't fully understand due to lack of experience.

Similarly, young adults don't aspire to return to the days of their early youth, when they had a curfew and weren't free to make choices about how they allocate their money. Most of them wouldn't trade their positions as rookies in the adult world for a veteran tag with the teenagers. However, they often hope for a bit more understanding from older adults. They realize that while they are taking on more responsibility, they still have a lot to learn and may need a break from time to time to feel their youth again. Marketers need to understand these concepts so they can aim their efforts toward what each distinct group of Millennials aspires to have, create, and afford. Young people today don't live their lives in a box. They're more complicated than the generations before them and want to have a voice without always feeling the burden of participating in big decisions about spending and time management.

Answer: B. Refer to case study for actual statistics.

Part Three   Young Today, Grown Tomorrow

7

BuzzSpotting

Tween and Teen Trends That Will Change the Way We Live and Work

BUZZSPOTTER PROFILE

It's 3 PM, and Mark locks the door of his apartment on his way to class. MacBook Pro packed safely in his Kenneth Cole bag and iPod in hand, he heads out. He gets halfway down the hall before he remembers he needs to drop his most recent Netflix rentals—the first season of Grey's Anatomy *and the fourth season of* Lost—*into the mail bin. After his class, Mark meets up with some friends for a quick dinner at a new, organic quick-dining restaurant. After dinner, he heads to Pilates. It's just the pick-me-up he needs before starting his workday—at 9 PM.*

Working nine to five? At a desk located in an office building? For a flesh-and-blood boss? If new Millennials get to live and work on their terms, then these strictures are headed the way of the fax machine. Even in an uncertain economy, this generation wants to make their own rules; in 2010, 41 percent of college graduates turned down job offers. Millennials just can't see themselves working for companies they don't believe in just to have a job. Why should they have to? Weren't they raised by parents who made sure they knew what "winners" they were and that they always deserved the best? Millennial dreams don't include the safety net of company-funded health insurance and 401(k)s, most likely because their parents have seen so-called protection like that vanish into the thin air of economic uncertainty. Their children will not grow up automatically expecting such perks. To them, the once-cherished article of faith that an employer would take care of its own—into retirement and beyond—sounds like an ancient legend from a lost civilization.

Sure, it's easy to scoff at the notions of tweens and teens who think that they can start a web site and then sell it off for millions, or start a fashion line in their bedroom and market it through Twitter, or join with friends to create an app that no one else has imagined. But can we really roll our eyes? Fueled by *instanity* and the realities of new entrepreneurial possibilities, Millennials are basing their lifestyle expectations on what they see happening around them every day.

Spotlight: Tavi Gevinson

Gevinson is a 13-year-old fashion blogger who launched her blog, Style Rookie, in March 2008. But to simply call her a fashion blogger is not enough; Gevinson is indeed a style influencer. At a mere 13 years, Gevinson receives invitations to major designer fashion shows like Rodarte and Balmain, and she has been featured in *Teen Vogue, Interview,* and *The New Yorker.* One might think that she's a precocious stage kid, pushed into blogging by overzealous parents, but that couldn't be further from the truth. In fact, her parents found out about her blog only when the *New York Times* wanted to feature her, at which point she had some serious explaining to do! More than 50,000 people read Gevinson's blog daily, and she's found a nice niche for herself at an almost astonishingly young age. Like most Millennials, Gevinson won't be pigeonholed. She's not sure if she wants a career in fashion at all. Her self-proclaimed true passion? Rapping!

Every generation works and lives differently; however, it's becoming apparent that the new Millennials will be at the epicenter of one of the biggest shifts in how society conducts itself on the job and at home. The boundaries between these two worlds have been all but obliterated by technology; the definition of *success* is no longer carved in stone, and attitudes toward money—obtaining it, spending it, saving it—have been redefined as a result of a recession that has impacted this generation's coming-of-age.

Following are of some of the trends that support these notions, along with details about how they're creating a huge shift in the culture of how we make money and spend time.

1. *Fewer teens will choose a traditional four-year college, as it is proving to be a questionable return on investment.* In a recent survey done by online brokerage company TD Ameritrade, 36 percent of high schools students claimed that they would delay or forgo college due to costs.[1] Young Millennials—and parents who foot the bill

for increasing costs that are out of proportion to their household incomes—look around and realize that they don't need college educations to think and act like entrepreneurs. Even those who do wish to pursue additional education opt increasingly for specialized training in areas like technology, the arts, the health care field or specific business fields.

A college education—namely, a bachelor's degree—used to be the foundation for a guaranteed career path, a tool that formalized the graduate's work life soon after graduation. It was a safe investment that essentially promised a chance for a solid return in the form of a fairly well paying job and some financial security. But as the population grows and the job market downsizes, there is upward pressure placed on the type of educational background that provides a foundation for success. This has resulted in the need for students to pursue advanced degrees such as MBAs and JDs. Nowadays, even advanced degrees have their career limitations. None offer an absolutely fail-safe return on the student's investment in education—an investment that has increased due to higher tuition costs and higher student living expenses. Millennials are countering this trend by reconsidering whether they even need a bachelor's degree to launch their careers.

In some ways, this idea isn't new. There are plenty of examples of extremely successful businesspeople who decided to forgo their college education to focus instead on building a business at an early age. Microsoft founder and CEO Bill Gates, certainly one of the most successful businesspeople in modern history, is one such case. A more recent example is Facebook founder Mark Zuckerberg, who decided to drop out of Harvard (coincidentally, Gates's former educational home) to launch his now extraordinarily popular social networking site. What used to be a rare occurrence is now becoming increasingly popular due to the simple fact that it's increasingly less difficult to become successful these days. The Internet has made it easier than ever for self-made professionals to get started by providing a plethora of low-cost (and even free) applications for basic business functions and quick access to valuable information. This allows young entrepreneurs, who are more fluid with online applications than their older, already-in-the-workforce counterparts, to develop their ideas to fruition without a major upfront investment in time or money.

Looking at the world through the eyes of an entrepreneur is now the rule rather than the exception for Millennials. This is causing a cultural shift as young people, armed with the tools to create and organize, are starting to monetize their hobbies by simply setting up a web site and registering as a company using resources such as Legalzoom.com. They're realizing that, regardless of whether they decide to pursue a higher education degree, starting a company—and learning to think like a businessperson—is the *real* investment, and the one most likely to pay off in the long term. Perhaps most important, these young people see the value of investing in themselves instead of in someone else's company or even an academic institution.

When we envision these self-employed Millennials, we usually picture the kind of individuals who end up on lists like *Inc.* magazine's 30 Under 30 or the "Young Millionaires" list from entrepreneur.com. But that's not necessarily who Millennials are thinking of. Instead, they're visualizing people like pop-singer-turned-style-mogul Jessica Simpson, who oversees a fashion label with nearly $500 million in annual sales, or someone like rapper 50 Cent, who reportedly made over $100 million when Vitamin Water, a company in which he invested, was sold for billions.

Both are prime examples of the positive impact of celebrity. Millennials are watching their icons run businesses, design, create, and innovate—and make tons of money doing it. They're learning some important lessons from these wealthy entertainers: You have to do multiple things to live the fabulous life, but you *can* make your fortune doing something you love. You don't have to be tied to a traditional, 40-hour-per-week job. You can make your own path and find success. And let's not forget that the majority of the celebrities they revere aren't traditionally educated. I'm not saying that they haven't earned an education in their own way; many simply have shunned the traditional system.

2. *Young people are more often working for themselves or in small collectives instead of heading for corporations, in part because they want to be their own bosses.* As I mentioned previously, technology has given this generation an opportunity to start businesses with little or no up-front investment, and at a very young age. (I should

know—this is how I started out!) Modern online tools provide ripe opportunities for entrepreneurs of all ages and often level the playing field in many industries. Younger people's ability to develop a speed and skill advantage on computers and the Internet in general gives them a leg up on their competition. For this reason, the ones who spend more time learning how to use their WordPress or Drupal (both are free and open source) web sites' content management systems (rather than trolling their Facebook news feed) are going to make some money. It will become gradually less common to meet people under 20 who haven't either started their own business or at least built their first web site. Since entrepreneurialism is addictive, once they dive in and learn to take a few risks, they'll keep manifesting their ideas into viable businesses as they get older and more experienced. Accordingly, the Millennial generation is likely to become the largest generation of entrepreneurs since the Industrial Revolution.

Although these technical tools and the current business climate present opportunities to ambitious and creative young people, the most prominent reason for the surge in young entrepreneurship is fairly straightforward: Millennials would simply rather work for themselves than anyone else. Corporate ladders are a thing of the past and provide less financial security than ever before. Millennials know more about successful businesspeople and entertainers than they do about the CEOs of Fortune 500 companies. They have access to books and articles written by prosperous entrepreneurs; they peruse small business and tech start-up blogs more frequently than the *Wall Street Journal*. In short, they're able to read the autobiography of a self-made millionaire like Richard Branson and learn straight from the horse's mouth. On the other hand, corporate CEOs seem to spend more time shuttered in their offices or testifying in front of Congress—providing a fairly bleak example of that particular career path.

Of course, one of the most common barriers to starting any business is amassing capital. But today's young entrepreneurs, especially the ones whose ideas are focused on the Internet, can launch these companies for minimal start-up capital and have maintenance costs that will diminish over time—providing real potential for return.

By contrast, college degrees, even some advanced degrees, no longer hold the shelf life that they used to, and many of them come encumbered with risky debt, much like the subprime mortgages of the past 10 years. We all saw how little those mortgages paid out to their investors, often providing massive headaches instead of healthy returns. By starting a company at a young age and giving themselves adequate time to learn the ins and outs of the business world, these young people actually *reduce* their risk of financial insecurity while building assets with the potential to create residual revenues over time.

This recession has only strengthened the allure of self-employment and small collectives for Millennials. However, an idea is worth nothing without action. Many economists wonder whether this generation as a whole has what it takes to actually realize dreams of entrepreneurship and small business management as a standard. Kevin Hempel, a consultant at the Children and Youth unit at the World Bank, cites several reasons why we should be cautious about the spread of entrepreneurship and the idea that self-employment can solve the youth unemployment crisis (around 20 percent of American youth are currently unemployed). Hempel first points out that many entrepreneurs fail in their first go-round, and sometimes several times after that. As obsessed as they are with the notion of *instanity*, do Millennials have what it takes to stick it out? Second, self-employment is born out of necessity in developing countries, and the same is often true in developed countries like the United States. For example, I started my company when I was 16 because I loved pop culture, but I also loved clothes. As the oldest of six children (with two hardworking parents in a normal, middle-class family), I knew my parents couldn't care less about my passion for fashion, because they needed to feed, clothe, educate, and emotionally care for our small basketball team. I used my wits to figure out how I could satisfy my craving for clothes, and I didn't really think twice about making money. Finally, running a company requires a certain set of skills that Millennials may not have yet required, such as accounting and human resource management.

Although Millennial entrepreneurship will most likely increase, the odds are that small collectives, in which members of this generation can utilize the overall group's best skills, will be the biggest area of growth over the next ten years. Working in small peer groups with people they trust seems like the best bet. Since Millennials won't take just any job that comes to them, collaborating with friends is a practical option.

3. *Millennials will work when and where they want to.* The virtual office is already a reality for many, a trend that will continue upward as technology transforms the workplace. As I've pointed out previously, while older generations had to *adapt* to technology, Millennials are making *technology* adapt to their needs and desires.

Nowadays, most of us complete business-related tasks on a computer—and often online. Virtual collaboration tools, document storage and sharing, videoconferencing, and real-time chat are all well past the beta stages of development and provide a solid platform for entrepreneurs armed with only their creativity and a laptop. It's no secret that we'd all prefer a flexible work schedule that allows us to keep our own hours and be more accommodating with vacation and family time. Millennials have heard older generations gripe about time wasted on long commutes and putting in 12 hours at the office with no break, only to have to go back in on the weekend to meet a deadline. They argue, and rightly so, that conventional methods are no longer the most efficient and economical ways to operate a business. They instead choose to develop companies from the ground up by keeping overhead low and engaging with customers by e-mail, and even via social media networks.

Virtual businesses also influence accelerated growth for international business opportunities. A teenager with a web site based out of his or her California home, with an Indian technical support staff and global customers, is very likely to learn quickly and on the fly about foreign cultures and international commercial laws through everyday experience. This type of knowledge was once exclusively guarded by small groups of jet-setting executives who managed behemoth corporations. Now, groups from all ages and cultures are attending business meetings together, either in the same room or via videoconference from London to San Francisco. The fact that younger people are so open-minded about this method of doing things marks a permanent shift in the global business culture. In fact, younger people consider the global market potential for a business idea first when writing their business plans, rather than starting with their local market and then expanding outward.

In Chapter 8, we explore a new trend I call *global mobiles*, a category into which most Millennials fall because they're living their lives without restrictions of locality. This further empowers Millennials to build global teams of peers around a central thought or idea. They won't be restricted by time zones to do that kind of work.

There is some concern that promoting virtual working environments will result in lower productivity due to lack of structure and that the virtual movement will cause more harm than good; however, these objections are becoming less prevalent. The truth is that allowing people to have more control over their time and location generally makes them happier and more balanced and gives them a chance to mix in some entertainment and social activities. Young people don't want to become like the bleary-eyed parents they see arriving home from the office late and missing their kids' sports activities. Therefore, they're getting a head start and taking advantage of the tools available for working in the virtual world.

Society has historically feared change—and this is a big shift that's threatening to take place in the workaday world. Yet it's highly probable that Millennials will be more productive in less time than their predecessors. For one thing, they don't place restrictions on their work life; there is no "nine to five" in their world. However, this doesn't mean that they define themselves through their careers—quite the contrary, actually. That's the very reason so many Millennial graduates turned down job opportunities in 2010: They refuse to be defined by a job. If a career opportunity doesn't reflect how they see themselves, then there's little chance they will take the opportunity. You might assume that they'd be concerned with earning a living; however, unlike other generations, this is their first experience with a bad economy. It is scary to think about what might happen when Millennials lose some of their optimism. Let's just hope the economy improves before we have to find out.

4. *This generation will work hard for their money and in turn will want value for the money they spend.* The cost of living keeps heading in only one direction; the job market holds ever more hurdles; and the economy continues to bubble. Because today's tweens and

teens are growing up with a more cautious approach to spending, marketers will have to fight harder and be more creative to attract these consumers as they age into adulthood.

The parents of Millennials grew up during a time of the greatest economic prosperity and growth in global history. They assumed that business would always get better and that upsizing the family home could happen every so often. They used credit and debt mechanisms to provide greater liquidity based on these assumptions. Then the sudden economic reversal put the brakes on this way of thinking. Young Millennials, like those who grew up during the Great Depression, were immediately inundated with a poor economic outlook and news that the days of care-free spending were over. Jobs became scarce commodities for young people and adults alike.

Not only did this economic shift cause more young people to consider entrepreneurship, it compelled them to focus more intently on the value of a job—and therefore the value of the dollar—whether they worked for someone else or created a position for themselves. They're no longer asking their parents for extra pocket money; instead they rely on becoming better at budgeting their own money in order to live the lifestyle they desire. Credit cards are staying in the wallet, cash is king again, and Millennials are counting their pennies. It has now become cooler to brag about what a great deal you got on a pair of sneakers than to wear a new pair of Gucci loafers with a flashy price tag. Don't get me wrong, those Gucci loafers are still cool, but you get more cool points if you picked them up on TheOutNet.com or Gilt.com.

Spotlight: Gilt Groupe

Launched in 2007, this online retailer offers "flash" sales on luxury men's, women's, and children's fashion items that usually last between 36 and 48 hours. The company was founded by DoubleClick cofounder Kevin Ryan, Italian jewelry company Bulgari merchandiser Alexandra Wilkis Wilson, and eBay

(continued)

(*continued*)

executive Alexis Maybank. Sales are announced via e-mail and usually start at 12 noon eastern standard time. Only current members can shop the sales, which feature brands like J Brand and Marc Jacobs. Members also receive a $25 incentive to refer friends, and they can use the discount toward an item of their choice when the friend makes a purchase. With a reported $200 million in sales in 2009, Gilt has also launched the successful site Jetsetter.com—the place to go for vacation deals (or steals, depending on how you look at it). Gilt's success makes you wonder whether consumers just wait for items to go on sale instead of buying it in the store. Either way, the site has forever changed lunchtime for millions of consumers.

Marketers have to pay attention and remain focused on the correlation between value and price. Dressing from head to toe in designer duds is not the Millennial way. Sure, brands like Gucci and Louis Vuitton continue to be hot with Millennials, but they are just as likely to purchase fashion items from Target and Walmart. What matters most is style, which is now a very affordable luxury. Young people scrutinize the message behind the brands they support. Much as a businessperson does a background check on a potential partner, they demand more transparency with regard to price, because they're learning, at an early age, about key areas of commerce that affect price—from outsourcing to supply chain management.

We've seen what happens when Millennials demand more value for price; just consider the great fall of the recording industry. Consumers insisted on receiving better value for the $17 they were forced to pay for a music CD that usually featured only a few great songs out of 11 or 12 total (though exactly which few qualified was obviously up for discussion). Enter iTunes and numerous other services, and consumers can now cherry-pick their music selections. This has resulted in a major industrywide loss of profits, as well as an estimated loss of 600,000 jobs.

What's happened to the music industry is just an example of the many casualties to come if marketers aren't smart about their value propositions. Remember, there must always be value. You might get away with inflation for a while, but it will even out at some point. In the past, record industry magnates could charge whatever they wanted for CDs, because they controlled the method of consumption (i.e., the way in which consumers could access the product). That control allowed them to charge a premium price, even when purchasers didn't feel they were getting the full value. Technology created the solution that consumers had been waiting for. Though buyers initially used illegal file sharing to access music, they have shifted to downloading it legally with ease. A 2002 poll of our buzzSpotters revealed that 99 percent admitted to illegally downloading music within the previous 30 days. By 2010, only 26 percent were still doing it.[2] Since consumers do see value in music, they will purchase it—as long as they can do so via a method that's convenient for them. But they're not interested in owning something that they don't want.

There are other examples of controlled methods of consumption. Take, for example, buyers for department stores. There was a time when these buyers controlled everything we wore. While they still control, for some brands, what companies produce to be sold in department stores, this isn't the case overall. When brands like Steve Madden boast an online store that generates more revenue than any brick-and-mortar location, the power of technology—and online shopping—becomes clear. Gone are the days when buyers could control which shoes, jeans, or purses we have in our closets. Millennials have options, and because they're savvy shoppers, they will explore them.

Since today's new Millennials will head their own households within two decades, tomorrow's working families will look very different from today's. As both parents need and want to generate earnings, the number of two-income families will continue to rise. But if more people are working for themselves, when and where they want, it could shift the work/family balance in a very positive direction.

The phrase "work-life balance" has become overly used by people trying to describe their approach to managing both a professional and a family life. In most cases, it seems to come in that order: first work, then family. Millennials are more comfortable merging the two, aspiring to work from home more and create supplemental income streams that allow for more financial flexibility.

A typical workday used to go something like this: Wake up, have breakfast and a quick shower, then head to the office; maybe work out or run a few errands at lunch; then head home for dinner and try to relax a bit before bed. Most entertainment activities were saved for the weekends. Young people today have instead been constructing schedules that go a little more like this: Wake up, check e-mails and organize the day, enjoy breakfast while scanning their favorite blogs online (likely related to their business interests or industries), and start the workday online from home; after a shower and lunch, head to the gym for a while before meeting with a graphic designer (possibly from the other side of the world via an afternoon Skype call) who's working on some new Web design; at night, enjoy dinner out with their significant other before finishing the day with a final sweep up of e-mails and to-do list.

Evenings and weekends are no longer the only times that they'll choose to spend with their friends and families. Once Millennials have children and households of their own, they'll find ways to get in more quality time with the spouses and kids by crafting schedules that allow them to do their work when their spouses are available to watch the kids (and vice versa) or when most of the household is sleeping. Not only will their children benefit from more parenting and less time left to their own devices (especially in their earlier years), but the merger of work and home life may allow Millennials to spend more time with their spouses in a very dynamic way: They will get know each other on both a personal and professional level. There will be much less dissonance between their office and family life. When both spouses are working (to cover household expenses in tough economic times) from home, they'll have the opportunity to intimately observe how the other spouse handles his or her professional career and relationships. Bridging this gap between home and work will bring spouses closer and give them more time to develop meaningful relationships—with each other and with their children.

It's important for marketers to understand how Millennials will spend their time in the future. For example, will you buy subway advertisements that target rush hour traffic if there *is* no rush hour? Will you shift advertisements from stay-at-home *moms* to stay-at-home *parents*? Is there an emerging market for upgraded home offices? We've already seen a home-theater market explode for a generation of nesters. The same could happen for Millennials who choose to "pimp out their pads" instead of submitting to corporate life.

As professional situations continue to transform, there will be many emerging opportunities for marketers. There are communal work centers springing up in cities all over the country. It's the perfect solution for those who freelance or work alone but don't want to be at home all day. These office spaces, which can be rented by the month, day, or even hour, are becoming a hot commodity.

Consider the ways in which you can shift your current product offerings to service Millennials in the future. Imagine how you can cater to them by creating new services and products. If you're a fashion brand, for example, will you need to create collections that target people who don't work in a traditional work environment?

There will be so many emerging opportunities and new markets for businesses in the future. This shift in mentality will bring change, but the smart brands will adapt and will offer Millennials the products they desire.

Millennials will break out of the two-party political system. The Tea Party movement is only the beginning. In this age of constant communications, when candidates can shun well-established national media sources in favor of granting exclusives to little-known blogs, political power is no longer controlled by traditional sources. Millennials see few solutions emerging from the current political climate, which is fraught with complications and blame. Once again, technology is the tool that will further empower this generation to change the political world as we know it.

The need for more than two viable political parties is becoming greater than ever, as the national dialogue becomes more venomous and partisan. It is increasingly difficult to pin down a candidate's position on any particular matter of policy, since many are either cautious or misleading in their public statements for fear of being ridiculed by opponents and the media. They are then chastised when somehow they manage to express their true views in private. For young people new to the political process, it comes across as charades and fanfare—a noisy joke. However, Millennials are learning more about the way government works and American civics due to a wealth of information and tools available online. They are taking this knowledge, formulating their own opinions, and then searching for candidates who support them, instead of being fed a choice of only two positions on public policy. It's very much the same challenge companies are facing: how to change the way they push their products and services to younger customers and instead engage with them to pull them in. Politicians, too, must start to listen more than they talk.

President Obama focused heavily on social networking and viral information sharing when campaigning for the presidency in 2008. He hired Chris Hughes, one of the four Facebook founders, who was only 24 at the time, to help lead his digital campaign strategy. It obviously worked, as young people showed up to vote in record numbers. This taught us several critically valuable things about politics in today's information age. First, young people are actively engaged in the political process when politicians reach them through the communication methods they use every day. Second, social networking and collaborative tools are effective for creating conversations about serious topics, not just frivolous status updates on Facebook. Third, these technical tools have become the cheapest way to facilitate campaign strategies, as they're much easier to plan and implement than campaign flyers, cold calling, or even television ads, which all require a tremendous amount of money.

We can expect social networking to play a bigger role in the elections to come as candidates are forced to spread a broad message on their policies with leaner budgets. This will open up opportunities for candidates of lesser means to compete for higher political offices—hence the breakdown of the two-party system.

In addition to technology's implications for politics, we have to consider whether two parties (and therefore two general bases of opinion and policy) are sufficient to address the complexities of the modern world. Just as they're learning lessons in international business, younger people are becoming more knowledgeable about their government's functions. They realize that they have the ability to select their candidates without turning to the mainstream media for advice.

This generation, which gets just as much of its information from social networks and blogs as it does from 24-hour news cycles, is less likely to be influenced by negative television ads and instead focuses on Wikipedia profiles and YouTube video clips from a candidate's past. It is certain, and very advantageous, that these changes will make the political process more transparent. Though Obama was the first presidential candidate to really take advantage of this phenomenon, his successors will most certainly follow in his footsteps.

However, politics in the future won't just be about social networking. Because Millennials have been raised in an inclusive environment, they don't really understand the need to be so divisive. The idea that "my idea is the only right idea" doesn't resonate with this age group, which is why so many of them found President Obama so appealing. He talked about reaching across the aisle to Republicans, claiming that he wanted to be inclusive and work together. What he failed to realize is that others have to reach back. Millennials are sick of politics as usual, and they're also tough on the president they once supported so wholeheartedly. In a recent Buzz Marketing Group political survey, only 29 percent of our panelists felt that the president was doing a good job, and another 71 percent felt neutral or negative.[3] Mind you, Republicans did not fare any better. When asked whether Sarah Palin is a viable candidate for president in 2012, 71 percent of respondents said no.

It's clear that Millennials do not want more of the same. They have high expectations of their government and are more than willing to participate in the political process. They realize that the only way to improve the situation is to become involved. They might not happy with the president's progress, but 92 percent of them fully intended to vote in the midterm election.

Millennials realize that our current system is broken. Many older Millennials discuss the "media manipulation" of facts and the focus on unimportant issues in focus groups. They also see political commentators and pundits as entertainers, not as a major source of news. Members of this generation care about the issues that matter to them, and they realize that those issues will change as they age. The topics that will matter to them 10 to 15 years from now will differ greatly from what's on the political agenda today.

Green will no longer be a movement, it will be an expectation. Millennials will have lived most of their lives in an eco-conscious society by the time they're running the world. They will continue to think about how they can take up less space and conserve for future generations. But Millennials will also be practical. For example, their automotive needs will fall somewhere between a Hummer and a Prius. They won't see a need for such extremes, unlike older generations, who may have felt compelled to buy a Prius out of guilt. They will be responsible, but they will also enjoy their space. The same is true for housing. They may not want megamansions, but they won't be living like paupers, either.

As the media marketplace becomes flooded with information about clean energy and worries over climate change, more people are becoming sensitive about the potential excesses of burning ever-more oil and consuming ever-more electricity with no regard for conservation. We're all learning to live with less, and phrases like "carbon footprint" and "renewable energy" are becoming common.

Young people are taking these messages to heart and investigating how to integrate human life with the rest of nature rather than overwhelming the planet with waste. Millennials are also the first generation who will build entire business careers within the clean technology industry. Over the past four decades, we have lived through numerous periods of economic growth in the oil, financial services, computer technology, and housing industries. Alternative energy has emerged as the newest untapped market for potential growth, and it appears to have a long shelf life because of the returns it promises for both financiers and consumers of its products. Governments across the world recognize this trend and are investing heavily in developing alternative energy products and projects.

With a fresh viewpoint on cleaner living and plenty of policy decisions driving both public and private funds into the related industries, many Millennials will find themselves building careers by understanding both the science and business behind alternative energy. They view this as a win-win situation: They'll contribute to cleaning up the planet and prolonging human life while being compensated well for their skills in a growing industry.

As eco-consciousness becomes the focus of their professions, it will naturally carry over to their home lives. When searching for a place to live, they're more likely to rank energy costs higher than other amenities such as extra space (which has to be cooled and heated) and industrial-grade appliances (which use a lot of energy). They'll recycle more and drive more fuel-efficient vehicles, no longer because they feel like they should, but because they want to. Finally, as working from home becomes more prevalent and longer commutes become more expensive and environmentally unfriendly, we'll see Millennials choose to live in urban areas, where they'll be able to work from the neighborhood communal workspaces (which provide free Wi-Fi) and walk or take public transit more often. How and where they live and work will change as well. Architects are already designing the homes of the future. Although prefabricated houses (dwellings manufactured off-site in advance) have been attempted many times throughout history, without much success, they may be the design of the future. It certainly feeds the need for *instanity*.

Technology and easy access to it will also allow Millennials more choices when it comes to how and where they live. They may no longer have to choose between urban and rural dwelling. If they can get the high-powered Internet connection on their farm, they may not see a need to work and live near a major city. Technology, after all, is the mother of convenience.

There will be a major revival of traditional values. Millennials were raised by a generation of parents who were less religious than their own parents. As a result, many of these raised their Millennial children to be a lot less religious, and they allowed a lot more exposure to "bad behavior." For example, the FCC has lowered the standards for allowing foul language on TV over the past 30 years. There is a rock bottom, and we'll be hitting it pretty soon. Millennials will crave the chastity they never had. There will be a revival—literally.

Just as Millennial economic habits will more closely reflect those employed during the Great Depression rather than those of the generations in between, old-school moral views and family values will also make a comeback. We've seen time and again that these two areas of life—money and values—are tightly intertwined. When children learn the value of a dollar, they often become responsible adults, because they understand how to manage their money for the benefit of those around them, usually their families. Kids who are raised under the assumption that the economy will always grow and jobs will always be available are naturally less inclined to manage their personal affairs tightly.

The notion of family in and of itself is continuing to evolve as well. Church attendance continues to decline, and the concept of marriage receives skeptical reactions due to well-publicized high divorce rates and nasty public spats when celebrities split up. This type of behavior has a tipping point. Millennials are unlike their parents in that they're more reluctant to rush into marriage for fear it won't last. They simply may not think they have enough money to build a solid foundation for the relationship, and they no longer feel generational pressure to get married and start a family. And because so many Millennials have grown up in single-parent households and felt the economic and emotional effects of divorce firsthand, they tend to take their romantic relationships more seriously.

New perspectives on privacy also influence how Millennials choose to act, both at home and in public. When the extramarital affairs of major celebrities and athletes are exposed, the stigma follows them for the rest of their public careers—and often for the rest of their lives. They become known for having cheated on their spouse rather than as a great athlete. Often, those who portray an inauthentic clean image are the most harshly penalized in the court of public opinion. Social networking and the wealth of personal information on Facebook and other web sites create the same type of public judgment in local communities. A person who is married with children and exhibits the photos and wall posts to prove it on Facebook will find it much harder to go out on the town and engage in infidelity. In other words, double lives are a thing of the past. Millennials will continue to learn from the mistakes of public figures who have been photographed, then ridiculed, for embarrassing public actions and infidelity.

Millennials are also withdrawing from traditional religion and instead embracing spirituality in their own way. Whether it's through yoga, meditation, or something entirely new, members of this generation crave a spiritual experience. It might even come through music or the arts. Millennials will create their own set of values. As an age group who enjoys the benefits of equality that previous generations fought for, Millennials will pick and choose their new battles. At this point in time, for example, the fight over the rights of same-sex couples is still ongoing. Millennials have grown up in an era of same-sex couples parenting their friends, as well as racially diverse communities. Because of this, they don't really relate to stigmas attached to pregnancies out of wedlock and explicit sexual activity. Still, their current feelings about all of these things may change in the future, when they choose to bring their own children into the world.

All of these trends have something in common. They touch directly on parts of our culture and daily lives that are essential to our existence: how we make and spend money, how much time we spend with our loved ones and friends, how we treat the planet on which we live, and, ultimately, how we treat each other. Millennials are feeling their way through current problems just like everyone else. They may seem scattered and even a bit radical at times, but they're going to put their modern experience to use when it comes time for them to handle more responsibility.

See that kid out there walking home from school, lugging a 40-pound backpack and clutching a cell phone? He was raised on organic baby carrots from Whole Foods, but now subsists on fries and soda when his parents aren't looking. His first car seat was in the back of a Ford Explorer, but Dad ditched it for a fuel-efficient Honda Fit. His mother made sure he always had plenty of books, but now he does most of his reading online, when he bothers to read at all. He might go to college, he might not . . . but still, this bundle of contradictions will someday have a mortgage, a car payment and offspring of his own. He'll be more involved in child care than his dad was, particularly if he works from home as his own boss. He may not be sure what he wants to do for a living, but he knows he wants to work for himself. He will eventually ditch junk food for a more fuel-efficient diet and will buy his own kids organic baby squash. And he will probably realize that there are good books to read, even if he downloads them onto his e-reader device.

Along the road to adulthood he may stop to get a tattoo or make a YouTube video of himself playing a Jeff Beck guitar solo. However, chances are he'll mature into a grown-up, free to make his own decisions as a consumer and as a private citizen. Pay attention to the choices he makes today; he's already making an impact on tomorrow.

Although the strength of that impact may still be unknown, marketers must do everything in their power to understand who this ever-changing consumer will be. This is an ongoing study; it's the project that never ends. Though Millennials are often called elusive and fickle, they are really just great adapters. They're always acclimatizing to the ever-changing world around them. Their lives and their world are moving fast. They're constantly trying to get a handle on what to do and how to do it.

Instead of trying to answer every question out there, focus on the ones that haven't even been asked yet. In Chapter 5, we took a look at classic brands that have been able to stand the test of time. What is the secret to their success? Well, they figured out how to walk the tightrope of maintaining their brand statement and philosophy while adapting their communications to their emerging and changing target markets. For the most part, the actual products haven't changed. A pair of Converse sneakers is pretty much the same today as it was 50 years ago. But the way a brand like Converse communicates with its customers has certainly changed and diversified tremendously.

I love the phrase "the more things change, the more they stay the same" because it's so very true. Consumers will always seek engagement with the brands they love. The question of what that engagement is and how it will happen is constantly up for discussion. The key is to realize that no matter what, brands matter—and Millennials love them. The future might look scary, but it's full of possibilities.

Marketing Moment: Even in this culture of *instanity*, we still need to take a moment to think ahead and plan strategically.

TINA'S TOP 5

1. *Fewer Millennials will choose a traditional four-year college, as it's proving to be a questionable return on investment.* This is actually good news for community colleges, technical schools, and certificate programs. Millennials will be educated, but how they pursue that education will be different in the future. Online universities, such as University of Phoenix, will continue to increase in popularity. Traditional colleges will have to expand and innovate to attract students.

2. *Increasingly, Millennials will work for themselves or in small collectives, as opposed to heading for corporations, in part because they want to be their own bosses.* Millennials have watched their parents work for years in corporations, only to have their security blankets ripped from them. They don't believe in big business, and they have watched the nontraditional successes of many contemporaries. The future may hold the same amount of solo entrepreneurship that exists today (around 20 percent), but there will be major growth in the area of collectives.

You will also see an increase in business services designed to cater to these collectives. Work space alternatives, health care alternatives, and virtual staffing needs will all be on the increase.

3. *Millennials will work hard for their money and in turn will want value for the money they spend.* Millennials grew up in good times—actually, great times. They've watched what happens when you spend excessively. Millennials will always be smart and educated consumers, and they will always consume plenty of stuff, but the big issue at play is value. Branding and imaging will no longer be enough to convince Millennials to purchase your goods. Even established brands will have to offer a very strong value proposition in the future.

4. *Green will no longer be a movement; it will be an expectation.* It is still very expensive to go Green. Once Millennials are in

(*continued*)

(*continued*)

charge, however, Green will be a way of life. Better systems will be in place, and a Green lifestyle will be attainable for all.

I also believe that this generation as a whole will take up less space. Monster cars and monster homes will be a thing of the past. Millennials will live well, but they won't live in exorbitant excess.

5. *There will be a major revival of traditional values.* We're living in a time where everything and anything goes. Because of technology, Millennials have access to all types of content. The acronym NSFW (not safe for work) is all too-well known among Millennials.

While they may not turn to traditional religion like their boomer parents, they will definitely turn to spirituality in some way.

8

The Coming of the Global Mobile

How the New Millennials Will Shape the Future

BUZZSPOTTER PROFILE

Anna opens up her laptop and logs on to Skype. She's been looking forward to her daily chat with her boyfriend Chris. Anna is currently teaching in Korea, so it's hard to keep in touch with Chris, who lives in Kansas City. They met in college and really want to make it work. As Anna is waiting for Chris to log on, an e-mail pops up in her in-box. "Oh, he's so sweet," Anna thinks, as she clicks on the link to the mixtape Chris made for her on MixTape.me. Chris pings her on Skype, and they start what will be a long conversation. He reminds her to download the latest episode of The Office *(a show they watch together), and she puts on a pot of Nescafé Gold coffee. It is going to be a long night.*

Pop Quiz

True or False: IBM is one of the top three brands in the world.

Messages used travel via courier pigeon, and people used to travel via horseback. Both have long moved across waterways on boats. Then, about 200 years ago, steam-powered train travel was introduced and people have been moving faster ever since. The Industrial Revolution sped things up tremendously by introducing coal-burning engines on trains and boats and automobiles. And we started conveying messages via wire, telephone, and eventually fax. Before long, trains were hauling people across the United States (and Europe and Asia) efficiently. Technology and invention introduced all types of devices to record images and messages—namely, still cameras, video cameras, and phonograph audio recorders—and we started efficiently capturing content. This caused a continuing evolution of devices used to view the content: televisions, record/tape/CD players, videocassettes, and DVDs.

The jet engine and long-haul aircraft have made it possible for anyone to safely circumnavigate the globe in about 24 hours. Computers have become the portal through which content is most frequently viewed, forcing device makers to become more sophisticated; enter portable high-definition flipcams for both still and video recording, digital audio recorders and players that can fit in the palm of your hand (both with battery lives of five-plus hours), and a variety of combinations thereof on your mobile device (which also happens to serve as a telephone). Needless to say, the methods we use to travel and disseminate messages have developed immensely over the past 100 years; even the developments over the past 15 were hard to imagine only a few years before they occurred. We live in an age where any impediments to moving people, goods, and information (in every currently known format) are almost nonexistent. We can reach every point on the globe within a matter of days, at most, and can convey messages to anyone in the world instantaneously.

The selection of goods has become a digital process, with seamless and extremely fast distribution and purchase. We can also provide and receive these services via digital mediums, which has changed the way *all* businesses operate now compared to 15 years ago. One of the biggest areas of impact of the hyperspeed information age in a consumer-driven culture like the United States has clearly been in the retail sector. Consumers are no longer confined to a limited selection of goods, often chosen by a single buyer (or handful of buyers) on behalf of the local retail department store. The shopping experience has blown wide open; goods from all over the world are now available anywhere, elbowing out plenty of intermediaries in the process. This transformation presents plenty of opportunities for retailers as they go for a piece of global market share (literally); however, it also presents the substantial challenge of how to stand out in the crowd.

The Millennials have grown up this world of *instanity*, where information, photos, and prices (when they're shopping) are just one click away. They are also just a security checkpoint and a passport stamp away from almost anywhere in the world, where they can witness firsthand how cultures all over the globe listen (and create) their music and tuck their jeans into their sneakers. How are today's marketers supposed to keep up with that? How do you keep product available for online distribution when you're not sure what the next big thing will be—when a hot new item could explode overnight?

How do you know how much product to keep in local retail stores when more and more Millennials are shopping online? These supply and demand issues are just the logistical tip of the iceberg in a mountain of marketing issues.

There was a time when you could not have that cool pair of jeans that were hot in Switzerland (which you read about in your favorite fashion magazine) without having to wait a good six months. That's not true for Millennials. They don't even have to wait for a letter from a pen pal, much less any fashion item they want. Millennials aren't forced to be patient, because they have so many choices. We've discussed what technology and *instanity* have done for this consumer. But the underlying trend here stems from this idea of genuine globalization. It's a reality for Millennials. There is no *us* and *them*; it's really just a world of *we*.

Music (really, the arts in general) is one area that has played just as big a role as technology in bringing people together. Foreign films like *La Vie en Rose* are making stars like Marion Cotillard into American icons as well. And celebrities like Lady Gaga aren't just American personalities; they're global icons. There is a major cultural exchange taking place, and while technology may be the conduit, it's not just about technology. It has extended into a variety of other areas and industries.

Where do brands fit in? Believe it not, they're the most important piece to this puzzle. People might seem to scoff at brands, but in reality, they not only love brands, they *need* them. This is certainly the case for Millennials. I've stated time and again throughout this book that Millennials are drawn to brands and marketing; brands give members of this generation a sense of self. How these young people choose the items that align with their needs, wants, and desires is a different story. But the biggest brands, and the ones that make the most significant impact, truly have the potential to become global icons.

This chapter introduces the notion of *global mobiles*, which are exactly what Millennials are going to become in the following years. We also take a look at some brands that have done a great job of creating a global presence. While some of them are the usual suspects, there are always additional lessons we can learn from them.

There are things that *every* product or service can do to make itself more appealing on a global level.

First, you have to create a brand with global values. For example, we know that *Warholism* is a major trend in the United States, but is it also taking hold abroad? Is reality TV as big in other countries as it currently is here? These are questions you have to ask. What are examples of global values? Things like love, happiness, style, and convenience all play on a global landscape.

Second, you must have a recognizable logo. Think about the companies that consistently make it onto Interbrand's list of the top 10 global brands: Coca-Cola, IBM, Google, Microsoft, and McDonald's, to name a few. All have recognizable symbols. Think about what your logo signifies to people all over the world. While product names are another element, this area is less restricted since it's the brand identity that matters most. I love the oft-cited marketing case study of the Chevy Nova, which supposedly sold poorly in Spanish-speaking countries because *no va* literally translates to "no go." The truth, however, is that the Nova actually performed quite well in some Spanish-speaking countries, such as Argentina, Mexico, and Venezuela. While it's great marketing fodder, it's simply not a true story. The truth is that more attention needs to be paid to overall branding approaches, since (as I've said several times before) brands that focus on creating loyal groups of consumers and on providing product value can pretty much get through any crisis, complete with customer forgiveness.

Third, you should not even think about creating a global brand if your customers cannot instantly connect with you. This connection should happen through a company web site and social networking sites like Facebook, Twitter, Foursquare, Clikthrough, and whatever other online experience is hot at that time. If you want to be global, you must be instant; there is no getting around this. However, an important distinction is that being instant doesn't mean that you can't be *exclusive*. Just look at a brand like Louis Vuitton. It's extremely exclusive; it's even been known to allow only a few people into its stores at a time! The company sells its products at select retail locations, and it produces only limited quantities. Yet the brand is everywhere—Twitter, Facebook, and, of course, the company web site. Louis Vuitton spokespeople are athletes, models, activists—people from every walk of life. This company understands the art of the global connection.

The fourth point for global brands to keep in mind is that traditional retail locations may not offer you the best solution. Pop-up stores are becoming increasingly popular these days, which might be an effect of the recession, since many malls and shops have tons of empty, available spaces. However, these stores aren't limited just to malls. Magazines are taking advantage of the trend as well, and publications like *Teen Vogue* and *Self* are providing brands with opportunities to interact with their consumers in new and exciting ways. Trade shows and live events also allow consumers to interact with the items that they love. Remember, it's about the connection, not just the visit to a traditional store.

Finally, you have to look for trends globally, not just what's happening in New York or California. The key to successful brands like Coca-Cola and hip retailer Urban Outfitters is that they are able to track trends globally while applying that information locally. A brand like Abercrombie & Fitch, for example, which is losing some of its U.S. popularity, has found a loyal fan base abroad, where the all-American look plays well. Similarly, this country has imported many of its favorite reality shows from abroad; *American Idol*, *Dancing with the Stars*, and *Big Brother* were all launched in England before they were hits in the United States. We even see some universal, cross-cultural values in these shows. Whether you're American or British, you still love dancing, singing, and family. These have global appeal.

Now that we know what matters, it's important to explore how this new breed of Millennials—or *global mobiles,* as I like to call them—will buy and consume products. It's equally important to know which brands are on their radar.

Global Mobiles

Today's youth are truly global mobiles, a moniker they've earned because, unlike any generation before them, they live in a world without geographic or cultural boundaries. They may start their mornings listening to reggae, buy their clothes online from Japanese clothing company A Bathing Ape, and use Netflix to watch foreign films—all within a few hours. Essentially, there are no limitations. With eyes wide open, their minds are wired to process all that they see, much like the computers and devices that consume the majority of their waking hours. Sound scary? Maybe, but the possibilities being created constantly among the minds of the world's youth are fascinating—and coming at warp speed. In the past few years, Millennials have produced the youngest billionaire in the *world* (not just in the United States), Facebook founder Mark Zuckerberg. Their work in the 2008 presidential campaign encouraged a global discussion about America's policies and future and led to the election of President Obama (who spoke in front of a crowd of more than 200,000 in *Germany* a few months before he became president). Millennials are changing the way the world thinks and communicates on a daily basis.

In a day and age when you hear so much on the news about international economic summits and the global economy, you can bet that Millennials, especially the older subsets, are paying attention. They're very informed about wars and ongoing struggles with countries like Iran and North Korea. And they're getting their information from what some might consider the unlikeliest sources. For example, *Vice* magazine, which focuses on pop culture topics—but has switched to covering more serious matters as of late—has a 13-webisode documentary series on North Korea. As far as many Millennials are concerned, the content they find on *Vice's* online network VBS.tv is more informative than anything they might watch on CNN.

The shopping experience has not just changed since Millennials came on the retail scene, it's essentially been revolutionized. This generation has experienced a complete restructuring of how we all spend money, and they are often on the front lines of new efforts for transformation. A trend that a teen in one part of the world spots is instantaneously adopted by another who is tens of thousands of miles away—whether it's the latest style of Nike skateboarding shoes or the wearing of the traditional Arab headdress known as a *keffiyeh* (a controversial political statement to some, a world-friendly fashion choice for others). *Gossip Girl* has leaped across the pond to become a big hit in the United Kingdom, while the British singer/songwriter Mika has headed thousands of miles west of London, gaining a huge cult following in the United States, thanks to none other than that one-man media blitz Perez Hilton (who himself was once merely a young twenty something blogging from his bedroom). Indeed, no blogger has had as big of an influence on global pop culture as Perez Hilton (aka Mario Lavandeira). His cultish blog, PerezHilton.com (his name is a playful knockoff of celebuntante Paris Hilton's), covers celebrities and events all over the globe. If it weren't for PerezHilton.com, stars like Minka and Cheryl Cole would be known only in Europe. Love him or hate him, Hilton has played a major part in countless celebrities' careers and has had substantial authority in creating their global appeal.

Younger Millennials are exerting considerable influence as well. Tavi Gevinson (introduced in Chapter 7) writes a blog called Style Rookie, which enjoys a substantial global following. What other 14-year-old girl might find herself at the Chanel show in Paris chatting with German fashion designer Karl Lagerfeld? When Gevinson blogs about the brands that she loves, she's not talking about typical teenage stuff: Serious fashion labels Rodarte and Comme des Garçons are more her speed. Gevinson is most certainly a global mobile.

Millennials are accustomed to observing a trend from abroad (either in person or virtually) or creating a new one by scanning real-time information from across the globe. This inherently and constantly affects their preferences in small but powerful ways. They don't want to be force-fed any preexisting ideas; they'd rather contribute to a new movement in other ways. For example, they'll show their support by purchasing products and touting those products to friends online. As Millennials continue to push for shopping in a digital realm, they are forcing retailers to "virtualize" their shopping experience. Even when young people decide they need to go to brick-and-mortar stores to pick up something, it's very likely that they at least "tried on" a few things from home before showing up. In this way, all storefronts now have same street address—and they all start with www.

We have to think more deeply about the current culture merge to understand how to market to Millennials. The underpinnings of culture are always found in human interaction—the communication within their relationships. The world's size used to be a mystery; even after it became finite (thanks to ocean explorers and eventually satellites and space travel), it still had a somewhat mystic quality to it. Now the Internet, along with increased international travel, has demystified this fog and connected us all with the speed of broadband and burning jet fuel. Millennials see the world as big, yes, but ever-so-portable, connected, and easy to navigate—either online or on foot (with a backpack and a smartphone loaded with travel apps). The tools to both learn and travel more quickly than ever have created an unprecedented movement of *transculturalism*, defined as "the merging and converging of cultures."*

With more than 500 million Facebook profiles from across the globe from which to browse, we're able to meet more people than ever. The relative ease of global travel—once a rare treat for most young people, but now a rite of passage for many—has made international relationships easy to develop and maintain over time, thus giving Millennials the opportunity to build business partnerships, find love interests, and make friends.

Families from Brazil to Belgium make international pilgrimages to the Apple Store on Fifth Avenue (and to the one in the Mall of America) to get their iPads, iPods, and iPhones. Although some American teens still get traditional summer jobs as lifeguards at the town pool, it's not uncommon for others to travel to a far-flung place like Senegal to teach English for the summer—and to meet new Skype video chat friends or a significant other while they're there. It was once considered exotic to host a foreign exchange student for a semester or to go to Latin America to learn Spanish; now, Millennials cross borders and time zones more casually than any generation before them. The influx of young immigrants to the United States from Latin America, Asia, and other places has also contributed to a new definition of "all-American kid." (According the Pew Hispanic

---

*Fernando Ortiz, a Cuban scholar and anthropologist who is credited with creating the field of AfroCuban studies, also coined the term "transculturalism."

Center, Latinos account for nearly a quarter of all American youth under age 18; Latino youth comprised only 2 percent of this group in 1980.)

Another interesting trend emerged during the recent recession. Some Millennials who opted out of a postcollege job decided to take a traditional gap year, some simply to go out and make the world a better place. There are dozens of programs looking for young twenty somethings who are eager to teach and make a difference in the world. Pause and think for a moment: Do you know one of them? We can probably all think of someone we know—sibling, colleague, child, cousin, friend—who has made the decision to live abroad for a year and whose global interaction touches everyone in his or her universe (thanks to Facebook). When these international ambassadors come home and tell everyone about the amazing things they've done and seen, it creates even more buzz about this type of experience. Global mobiles are true brand evangelists and ambassadors, and they are definitely shaping the world that all Millennials will inherit.

It's not uncommon for a Millennial to casually mention something like the following during a conversation: "My friend who is living in Milan right now is working on a solar-panel project with a new type of technology that's booming in Europe, and I've been thinking about going over there for a weekend visit." The borders that once separated countries have been replaced by an off-on switch on a laptop, the glow of a webcam, and an electronic boarding pass.

Now more than ever, Millennials have the tools, opportunities, ethnic diversity, and mind-set to become true citizens of the world. What will this world look like? How will this global-mobile culture impact our society? To answer these questions from a business marketers' perspective, let's take a look at a handful of global brands that are successfully reaching Millennials. Because of their upbringing and the skill sets acquired during the upswing of globalization, Millennials naturally expect marketers to connect with them on a global level while at the same time appealing to their local ideas. While this can be a tightrope for marketers to walk, some brands are doing it right.

I've given you a checklist of things to consider in your quest for world domination. Many of these to-do items have been gleaned from companies we're all familiar with that are doing an amazing job of targeting their customers on an international level. Though I've already discussed many of the following companies at length, I want to close this book by sharing some important lessons we can all learn from a sampling of these global power players. These companies, which many of us already know and love, offer brands that impact our lives every day. Whether stylish, inspiring, or practical, they are where every brand should desire to be—on top and making an impact.

Topshop

Topshop is largely responsible for bringing British ideals and high-street fashion to the United States at a reasonable price point. Millennials who seek to bring their level of sophistication up a notch appreciate London's high-street standards, such as fabulous frocks for $100 or less. Topshop has successfully created a virtual bridge between continental Europe, the United Kingdom, and the United States. However, Topshop hasn't always operated on such a global scale. The brand was founded in 1964 and launched within a department store. It branched into menswear in the 1970s by launching Topman, but was not necessarily considered a fashionable brand until the 1990s. That's when the company took the opportunity to reinvent itself, offering celebrity collections by models like Kate Moss and participating in fashion shows during London Fashion Week—the only high-street brand to do so. In fact, the London flagship store has more than 30,000 visitors each day.[1] Topshop operates stores in 20 countries, including Malaysia, Albania, Sweden, Russia, and the United States.

What is its major key to success? Like affordable U.S. clothing chain Forever 21, Topshop focuses on the notion of "fast fashion," evidenced by the fact that the chain updates its wares in its New York location *five times per week*. How's that for being in the moment? Topshop claims that one of its secrets to success is "capturing the zeitgeist every season." Whether sequins, hot pants, or jumpers are hot, Topshop has them. Delivering fast and trendy fashions is no easy task, and Topshop repeatedly offers this to its clientele.

American Express

Visa and Discover credit cards may heavily market to Millennials, but the card that resonates with them most is American Express, or AmEx, as many of my buzzSpotters call it. Millennials consider this to be one hot piece of plastic. And they're not the only ones who think so; *Fortune* magazine ranked American Express as one of its 30 most admired companies in the world in 2009.

Though founded in 1850, American Express did not enter the financial services business until 1882. The company actually functioned as an express shipping business during its first 30 years. Despite the transition to finance, it wasn't until 1957 that American Express entered the charge-card business. On October 1, 1958, it issued over 250,000 paper cards (plastic cards were not released until a year later). Since that time, the company has fully established itself as a major force within the industry, and it has constantly changed as the times have demanded.

It's clear, for example, that American Express knows a thing or two about the television business, based on its award-winning and captivating advertising campaigns like "Young Lawyer" (1986) and "Manhattan" (2001), but it's a little-known fact that AmEx was a cofounder of MTV, Nickelodeon, and The Movie Channel—all under the umbrella of Warner-Amex Satellite Entertainment, which was eventually sold to Viacom. While it may have taken American Express years to find its niche, its prominence as a global brand is colossal. AmEx has a card for every type of consumer. Do you love to travel? Well you should try the American Express Starwood Preferred Card. Opening up a business and just need a reliable credit line? Try the American Express Plum Card. Looking for bragging rights with your friends? Well then, the new Zync card might just be for you. It's ubiquitous yet exclusive, classic yet cutting-edge. American Express has fully mastered the art of tightrope walking.

Google

In a recent survey of our tween buzzSpotters to find out how they get information about new products, "Google" was second only to "friends" as a response. There is no denying that Google is a global giant. But you don't think of Google as sexy, thought-provoking, and creative. You most likely envision its practicality, and then you probably think about how many times you use it each day.

Still, Google has entered the same level of brand ubiquity as brands such as Xerox and Kleenex. Think about it: Do you search for things online? No, you "Google" them, in much the same way you might "Xerox" that document or ask for a "Kleenex." That sort of transcendence is very rare, and it has occurred because Google makes people's lives easier. Indeed, Google has made writing this book easier for me. With so much research and so many brands, Google became my sidekick—every few words! Global mobiles love Google. They need it, and it keeps them connected to the world just as much as their beloved Facebook. Google recently improved its search engine, and it's now easier to search words, images, and photos. Google mail, or Gmail, is also very user-friendly. Users are allotted plenty of mailbox space, and they can navigate multiple accounts with ease.

Nokia

Most Millennials recognize Nokia, not only because it is world's largest producer of mobile phones, but also because it makes some fairly distinctive, high-quality products. In addition, the company is a major player in telecommunications and even in computer software. Nokia describes itself as having a "flat, networked organization, as well as speed and flexibility in decision making." Nokia considers the critical elements in its process to be engagement, cooperation, innovation, and humanity. For example, Nokia engages with customers via its blog, Nokia Conversations. It's an exchange of ideas and thoughts, as well an idea center. There are even discussions about the future of technology and sustainability. This is a great example of how vital it is to have simple ideas that are global in nature. These ideals make sense for both employees and consumers.

While these may sound like lofty goals, keeping it simple has led to unparalleled success for Nokia. With the plethora of cell phones and providers from which customers have to choose, it's essential for brands in this industry to find a way to break through the noise. And, most of the time, the simpler the formula, the better.

Walt Disney

It's no secret that children love Disney, yet this brand has also figured out how to capture the hearts of people at every stage of their lives. My boomer parents still love Disney World; they vacation there without their six children!

There is so much that can be said and written about this brand and its founder, Walt Disney, concerning the reasons it continues to thrive. However, there's one area in particular on which every brand, emerging or not, absolutely must focus: original content generation. Everything within the Walt Disney Corporation is built around stories. They might be tales of princesses and wicked witches, children coming into their own, or even fashion, but there's always some kind of story there that resonates with millions of people. When most people envision Disney, they immediately think about imagination and good, solid storytelling. Dreams are powerful things, and Disney dares you to dream. That message resonates with people all over the world. For example, it prompts little girls everywhere to ask, "If an average girl can become a princess, why can't I?" All it takes is a little magic, or a visit to the (aptly named) Magic Kingdom. While Disney has had some struggles trying to bring its theme park concept to other parts of the world, the original is doing just as well as it always has. As long as people think and write (or type), they will dare to dream—and this will ring true for every generation to come.

Ikea

Show me almost any twenty something's apartment, and I'll show you at least one item from IKEA. This Swedish home-products superstore truly understands what matters to today's Millennials: style on the cheap. Even though IKEA does a great job of marketing to Millennials, it tends to let its products do the talking for the brand. Just as Topshop has emerged as a global fashion icon for budget shoppers, IKEA has firmly established its role as the stylish place to go for home interiors that won't break the bank.

Would you believe that a 17-year-old launched the world's largest furniture retailer? Indeed, Ingvar Kamprad (who grew up in Elmtaryd and was originally from Agunnaryd) was just as smart then as Millennials are now. The name IKEA is an acronym consisting of Kamprad's initials, plus the first letters of his hometown and the town in which he was born. Even the company name shows creativity!

Despite IKEA's widespread popularity in homes and offices everywhere, most people don't know that IKEA is ramping up its brand extensions. Already in the United Kingdom and Scandinavia, IKEA is expanding a concept called BoKlok—flat-pack houses. What an amazing concept for people who want to live an IKEA life! Like all other IKEA products, these homes are simple in design and very affordable. Additionally, in August 2008, IKEA launched a mobile phone network, called Family Mobile, in partnership with T-Mobile. The brand clearly understands that once you have a loyal following, you have to think outside of the box (literally!) and expand your products and services to fit consumers' needs.

Volkswagen

Volkswagen is hot with Millennials. According to *Forbes,* the Volkswagen Beetle is among the top five cars teens want. And models like the Golf, Jetta, and Passat are hot with Millennials, as well. Even though Volkswagens are a bit more expensive than the cars Millennials usually end up with (Honda, Ford), the company's marketing is spot-on. Volkswagen looks and feels like a Millennial brand. Even though it is selling a product that can be used by members of any generation, there's a feeling of fun associated with owning one of these cars. In fact, one might accuse Volkswagen of being *too* Millennial in some ways. The company seems lately to focus heavily on "aging up" to fit into the lifestyles of aging Millennials and their Generation X siblings. For example, its Touareg midsized SUV is positioned as a "premium SUV with the soul of a Volkswagen."

Volkswagen understands that it's not just selling cars: It's selling an entire brand experience. The cars are fun, fashionable, and valuable. While they might not seem like the most affordable option at first glance, they're certainly not as expensive as luxury vehicles. Volkswagen truly seems to be pioneering a class all its own.

McDonald's

McDonald's is consistently a thoroughbred type of company that always looks toward expansion while keeping on eye on the ground to make sure the golden arches are known for only one thing: the same quality and service, no matter where you find them. As the most recognizable fast-food chain, the brand has been under fire in recent years; it is commonly accused of being an "evil empire" by health-food fans. The brand nonetheless manages to maintain a loyal (and fairly massive) global following. Its products are amazingly consistent worldwide, despite some adjustments in serving sizes and flavoring.

Simply put, McDonald's has mastered the art of being a global brand with a local presence, making it a mainstay of American business and global culture—and a brand that will surely be adopted by generations to come. As the world's largest hamburger chain, McDonald's services more than 58 million customers each day[2] and operates 31,000 restaurants in 119 countries.[3]

Abercrombie & Fitch

One-time mainstay of everyday American fashion Abercrombie & Fitch (or just "Abercrombie," for short) has lost a lot of momentum during the past few years. But instead of panicking and sticking to what seemed to be its core customer base, the company went abroad to tap into the global marketplace. The brand quickly became popular with Italians, a culture that prides itself specifically on its sense of style. It turns out that Italians love the American aesthetic, which they had discovered in Polo prior to discovering it in Abercrombie. The company has found a way to exploit a global niche by peddling its line with a sense of "casual luxury," a trend that has turned out to be locally popular on a global scale.

Currently in the midst of a major global expansion, Abercrombie has flagship stores in London, Milan, and Tokyo, as well as in its home city of New York, with many more international locations planned over the next few years. It is a classic example of an all-American brand, founded in New York in 1892, that was able to shift with the tides of globalization and to share its version of casual luxury with the world.

What can marketers and other brands with global aspirations learn from these examples, and from the reactions of Millennials themselves? How have these companies positioned themselves today to keep up with tomorrow's global-mobile Millennial? And how do we translate what this generation is trying to tell us with the choices they make every day?

I think we've answered these questions. Every time you face a challenge, take some time to read about one of these brands (or make a list of your own) and see how they were able to face, and overcome, a similar obstacle. Marketers and brand builders in every generation have struggled with their own set of trials in their attempts to target to emerging markets; this is nothing new. The way in which we handle those challenges, however, differs across products, companies, and industries.

Chasing youth culture and getting it right is an ongoing discussion; it's something you have to do every day, not something you figure out and "finish" only one time. Customers are changing their minds every minute; however, they'll always need to purchase things. Your goal is to make sure it's *your* products or services that they're purchasing.

I feel extremely excited for the future when I reflect on this generation. I know that a lot of people are preparing themselves to deal with a generation of angst-ridden, entitled misfits. But I think we'll find our modern Milllennials to be thoughtful, careful, informed, practical, and brand-loyal.

In some ways, the recent recession has enabled us all to hit a reset button. Millennials (and members of other generations, for that matter) will spend money on their favorite things. They will not, however, just purchase something for the sake of purchasing it. You will have to work harder for their money. In their virtual playground, they will always be able to find something cheaper, better, and more stylish. The key is to figure out how you can connect with them in the realms and media in which they're most comfortable.

Millennials want a brand experience that is more involved than just coming across an ad in a magazine. Even though the music business is in serious decline (some even say close to its end), it still produces phenomena like Lady Gaga, an entertainer who offers fans an experience like no other. She is unique, she's talented, she's controversial, she's original—and she is the most downloaded artist in history. It *can* be done. The best brands will figure out how to get it done.

We're entering a time when brands need to listen more than they need to talk. What are consumers saying to you? What do they need from you now? What might they need 10 years from now? These questions should be top of mind every day. Whether your company is big or small, the answers will shape your future.

However, you can't answer any of these questions until you get to know your customer. If you don't like traditional research, do something on your own. Figure out a way to speak with your customers and find out exactly what they want from you. And don't talk with only them once; make it an ongoing process. Build panels and speak with them frequently. I can't tell you how much I learn through our research here at Buzz Marketing Group. It makes me laugh; it makes me sad; it makes me hopeful; sometimes it even makes me feel depressed. But it's a much-needed gut check, and it's not something I can get away with doing only every couple of months. I want to know what Millennials are thinking every day of every week.

I know this might sound like a pretty a tall order, but it really isn't: Get on Twitter and take a look at which items are trending. Go to the movie theater on a Friday night. Head to the mall (or Kohl's) over a weekend. Check out your local Starbucks around 3 PM. Youth culture is happening everywhere around you. You just have to stop and pay attention.

I advise all of my clients to get a small notebook and keep it with them at all times. Every time you see or hear something happening that inspires you, write it down. And refer to it often.

Once you're armed with information, it's time for innovation. And here's one thing you should always remember: Stay true to yourself and your brand. You know how low your prices can go if you're a luxury brand. I respect companies like Louis Vuitton that never have a sale and that, instead of slashing prices, create new points of entry for consumers with products below $200.

Even if you take all of my advice, you might still fail (just ask Martin + Osa). Only the strongest and the best brands will survive with Millennials. We've seen the vagaries of teen print media (e.g., *YM, Elle Girl, Teen People*), and failures will continue to happen in other industries as well. But we all learn something new from every endeavor—whether it succeeds or not.

To those nonmarketers who have survived reading this book, congratulations! I hope you've learned something about Millennials, and I hope that you are truly as hopeful and inspired as I am at this very moment. What Millennials need most is our support. We've given them the tools; now they need to build and create the next wave of global brands that people will love for the next 100 years.

So . . . what's next?

As much as he is talked about (like him or not), Mark Zuckerberg is truly the leader of the global mobile generation. One out of every 14 people on the planet is on Facebook. It's not just Zuckerberg himself, but the service he created that is the true model for the global mobile generation. Facebook incorporates all of the important values of this generation: It's instant, global, free, seamless, and connective. It's everything that matters to today's Millennials, and it's no wonder that there are more than 500 million members.

What is the key to chasing youth culture and getting it right? Don't assume that you, the marketer, business owner, parent, or interested observer, know everything. Chasing youth culture is just as much about observing as it is creating. Postrecession Millennials don't just need cool new products, they need solutions; they need combined products and services that will make their lives better. It can be something as simple as product X, which helps me communicate with my friends better, or product Y, which allows me to be trendy without spending tons of money. Or perhaps I love dealing with Company Z, simply because it has 24-hour phone support and someone always answers quickly. There is still, and there always will be, fundamental value in creating simple solutions. Focus first on the needs, then transition to the wants. Create your product or service for *tribes*, not just for demographics. Be disciplined in brand development, and think globally. Create things that matter and have value. If you can do this, you will get it right more often than you will get it wrong.

TINA'S TOP 5

1. *Create a brand with global values.* We've reached the pinnacle of a marketer's most fervent dream and worst nightmare rolled into one: Marketers are tasked with creating an image (via consistent campaigns) for a brand that the world at large will accept, while somehow still appealing to the community values found in its customers' local cultures. Though the potential for scaling a brand is greater than ever, and brand integration possibilities abound, consumers see the things they purchase through a filter of the world's cultural mix—a constantly churning stream of ideas and forms of expression. Above all else, it's important to recognize how people *feel* when they associate with a brand. Cosmetic tweaks, color schemes, and functional trends will always have their cycle, but longevity lies in the

(continued)

(continued)

ability of the world to understand the intention behind a brand's purpose. The globe likes to ask *why* a lot more than *what*, and brands must be able to answer this question.

2. *Focus on a logo that will appeal to Millennials globally.* The need for a remarkable logo to go along with branding and image elements is unquestionable. As is the case with almost any business, a distinctive mark that you can incorporate into designs for both style and recognition is a key element in establishing a global presence. Remember, this mark won't be used only to signify goods anymore; it will be stamped on various online messaging, may sit alongside assorted sponsorship partners for an athletic event abroad, and could easily be the favicon (i.e., favorites icon) and main button icons on a retailer's online shopping portal. As with simple products, simple logos have the longest shelf life.

3. *Remember that* instanity *is the key, and always be ready to answer the question: How can today's Millennials connect with your brand instantly?* A company with a sense of global awareness and an instantly recognizable logo will create instant connections between Millennials and that brand. This is where strategic marketing campaigns can provide the glue between the multiple impressions of the brand in front of Millennials in various settings. For example, a kid sees a pair of sneakers with a distinct logo on a passerby's feet. He recognizes it from an image on a friend's Facebook newsfeed from the night before. He pulls out his iPhone, opens up his friend's profile and searches through his wall posts until he finds the image. His friend has written the name of the shoe line in the description of the photo, so the kid Googles the name and goes to the brand's online shopping portal to check out colors and sizes. He also performed a local GPS search for retailers within walking distance that may have some shoes in stock. If the brand does not have a retailer nearby and is out of stock in his size and style, it has lost a sale.

4. *A traditional retail store is not always the answer. Pop-up stores are lucrative and mobile.* To create a local hand-to-hand feel, brands are slowly prying away from brick-and-mortar retail stores and ramping up campaigns for pop-up parties and events. The concept essentially reverses the traditional notions of marketing retail products, which was to set up shop in a neighborhood that seemed to cater to a particular sense of style and build a customer base locally, then regionally, then nationally, and so on. These days, technology has eliminated the need to invest in storefronts and instead allows both new and old brands to gather valuable data about customers' preferences and locations. With this knowledge so easily at their disposal, brands are able to home in and localize in geographic areas where they enjoy dense market coverage, and there host an event (basically, throw a party). These events provide seemingly endless cross-branding opportunities by combining fashion, music, technology, and even food into a true lifestyle experience. Companies can easily convert an event's content to an online format to let those who weren't physically there stop by and visit virtually from anywhere in the world.

5. *Look for global (not just U.S.) youth trends. Find the things that Millennials are doing (and buying!) today in London that could be in New York tomorrow.* Remember that today's youth are all connected. They listen to a lot of the same music and are influenced by the same television programming and movies, and they often discuss these topics in message boards and on the walls of Facebook profiles worldwide. This is where word-of-mouth buzz has gone from a chat on the corner in the neighborhood to e-mails from South Africa or South Korea. To that end, you must perform market testing on cross-cultural platforms that allow you to gather feedback from global resources and brand ambassadors all over the world.

Our buzzSpotters are the Millennial networkers; they've branded themselves from an early age as global mobiles. They

(*continued*)

(*continued*)

know what they like, and they study every piece of information they can get about it—whether it's fashion-, sports-, or entertainment-related—by starting with a simple Google search and ending with direct contact with a brand. They won't hesitate to send a cold e-mail to a boutique shop owner oceans away to ask about a price, customs taxes, and shipping fees. The distance isn't relevant to them—and it shouldn't be to brands, either. As trends develop globally, brands have to look for connection points to find the core group of customers who are going to help them cross borders easily and spread into new markets.

Marketing Moment: Marketers must acknowledge that today's Millennials live and think globally, even if they seem local.

True. IBM is the number two brand in the world, according to Interbrand's list of the top 100 brands in the world.

Notes

Chapter 4

1. From the KFF study on media consumption, "Generation M2: Media in the Lives of 8- to 18-year-olds," released January 2010.
2. From the survey,"*Teenagers: A Generation Unplugged*," released September 12, 2008, by CTIA—The Wireless Association in conjunction with Harris Interactive. More than 2,000 teenagers were surveyed about their cell phone habits in this study. A recent article in the *New York Times*, "Everyone's Using Cellphones, but Not So Many Are Talking," (May 16, 2010), cited CTIA figures on the increase in texting (up 50 percent in the past year).
3. From the Pew Study, "*Millennials: A Portrait of Generation Next,*" released February 2010.
4. From the Buzz Marketing Group Study, "*What Teens Want,*" released May 2010.
5. From the National Center for Educational Statistics Study, "*Teachers' Use of Educational Technology in U.S. Public Schools: 2009.*" Released May 2010.
6. From the Buzz Marketing Group Study, "*buzzOn Tweens,*" released April 2010.
7. MTV "A Thin Line Backgrounder," October 2010.

Chapter 5

1. Prendergast, Mark, *For God, Country and Coca-Cola: The Definitive History of the Great American Soft Drink and the Company that Makes It* (New York: Basic Books, 1994).
2. Pittsburgh Business Times; June 29, 2010.

Chapter 6

1. "Weekly Program Rankings". ABC Medianet. September 25, 2007.
2. "Broadcast TV Ratings for Monday, September 1, 2008". Your Entertainment Now wordpress.

3. http://tvbythenumbers.com/2010/06/16/final-2009-10-broadcast-primetime-show-average-viewership/54336
4. Ibid.

Chapter 7

1. From the TD Ameritrade study "2010 Teens & Money Survey," released July 2010.
2. From the Buzz Marketing Group Study, "What Teens Want," released May 2010.
3. From the Buzz Marketing Group Study, "buzzOn Politics," released October 2010.

Chapter 8

1. www.nytimes.com/2006/06/21/business/worldbusiness/21topshop.html
2. AFP, "McDonald's posts sizzling 80% profit rise in 2008," *Breitbart.com*, Retrieved August 27, 2010, http://www.breitbart.com/article.php?id=CNG.aec4920fe8094fdd0baaeab2ed126bf1.741&show_article=1.
3. www.mcdonalds.ca/en/aboutus/faq.aspx, Retrieved May 8, 2008.

About the Author

Tina Wells, CEO of Buzz Marketing Group, graduated with honors from Hood College in 2002 with a B.A. in Communication Arts. Currently a Wharton School of Business student for marketing management, Tina continues to create innovative marketing strategies for numerous clients within the beauty, entertainment, fashion, financial, and lifestyle sectors. Tina has worked with clients such as Maidenform, SonyBMG, PBS, Procter & Gamble, Sesame Workshop, and American Eagle Outfitters. Tina's long list of honors include *Essence*'s 40 Under 40 Award, *Billboard*'s 30 Under 30 Award, and *Inc.*'s 30 Under 30, to name just a few. She is the author of the tween series *Mackenzie Blue*, published by HarperCollins Children's Books, and *Chasing Youth Culture and Getting It Right* (John Wiley & Sons, Inc., 2011). Tina serves on the board of directors of the Philadelphia Orchestra Association, The Franklin Institute, and The Young Entrepreneur Council. She resides in Southern New Jersey with her vast collection of shoes.

Index